D0362845

Born in 1950, Rowan Williams was educated in Swansea (Wales) and Cambridge. He studied for his theology doctorate in Oxford, after which he taught theology in a seminary near Leeds. From 1977 until 1986 he was engaged in academic and parish work in Cambridge, before returning to Oxford as Lady Margaret Professor of Divinity. In 1990 he became a fellow of the British Academy.

In 1992 Professor Williams became Bishop of Monmouth, and in 1999 he was elected as Archbishop of Wales. He became Archbishop of Canterbury in late 2002 with ten years' experience as a diocesan bishop and three as a primate in the Anglican Communion.

Archbishop Williams is acknowledged internationally as an outstanding theological writer and teacher as well as an accomplished poet and translator. His interests include music, fiction and languages. But as archbishop his main responsibilities have been pastoral – whether leading his own diocese of Canterbury and the Church of England, or guiding the Anglican Communion worldwide. At the end of 2012, after ten years as archbishop, he will step down and move to a new role as Master of Magdalene College, Cambridge.

THE LION'S WORLD

A journey into the heart of Narnia

Rowan Williams

Illustrations by Monica Capoferri

First published in Great Britain in 2012

Society for Promoting Christian Knowledge
36 Causton Street
London SW1P 4ST
www.spckpublishing.co.uk

Copyright © Rowan Williams 2012
Illustrations copyright © Monica Capoferri 2012

Rowan Williams has asserted his right under the Copyright, Designs and
Patents Act, 1988, to be identified as Author of this work.

All rights reserved. No part of this book may be reproduced or transmitted in any
form or by any means, electronic or mechanical, including photocopying,
recording, or by any information storage and retrieval system,
without permission in writing from the publisher.

SPCK does not necessarily endorse the individual views contained
in its publications.

The author and publisher have made every effort to ensure that the external website
and email addresses included in this book are correct and up to date at the time
of going to press. The author and publisher are not responsible for the content,
quality or continuing accessibility of the sites.

Scripture quotations are taken from The New Jerusalem Bible, published and
copyright © 1985 by Darton, Longman & Todd Ltd and Doubleday & Co.,
Inc., a division of Random House, Inc. and used by permission.

British Library Cataloguing-in-Publication Data
A catalogue record for this book is available from the British Library

ISBN 978–0–281–06895–1
eBook ISBN 978–0–281–06896–8

Typeset by Graphicraft Limited, Hong Kong
First printed in Great Britain by Ashford Colour Press
Subsequently digitally printed in Great Britain

Produced on paper from sustainable forests

To Rhiannon and Pip, with all my love

Whereof we cannot speak,
thereof we must write children's books.

(Francis Spufford, *The Child that Books Built*)

Contents

Preface

I came late to Narnia; despite an obsessively bookish childhood in a Christian household, Lewis's books somehow
did not cross the radar until I had discovered his works of
apologetic as a teenager. I had read *The Screwtape Letters*,
Mere Christianity, *The Problem of Pain*, *Miracles*, *The Great
Divorce*, even *Letters to Malcolm*, before I knew much more
of the Narnia books than their covers. As a sixth former,
I discovered the *Preface to Paradise Lost* and the first
published volume of selected letters, a treasury for several
years to come. My initial reaction to Narnia was in fact
lukewarm, not helped by a rather lacklustre television version
of *The Lion, the Witch and the Wardrobe* in 1967, which
somehow made the theological message feel crudely obvious.
Discovering the books over again as a student, I realized that
what I had not registered was the wit of the actual writing
and the sheer psychological penetration of so much of the
character drawing. Above all, I found in them what I had
found here and there in *Screwtape*, in the astonishing achievement of *Till We Have Faces*, in *A Grief Observed* – a doorway
into a simple intensity of feeling about God that was able

both to register all the range of ambiguous and confused human feeling and still evoke an almost unbearable longing for that fullness of joy which Lewis points to so consistently in his best writing.[1]

He was, when I was first being educated as a theologian, a slightly embarrassing phenomenon (this at least is a thing of the past; we now have an excellent *Cambridge Companion to C. S. Lewis*, with contributions from some very formidable professional theologians):[2] someone who was read and circulated enthusiastically – if pretty selectively – by the sort of people who would be regarded as very unsophisticated by a proper theologian. I was given the grace to recognize that this kind of snobbery simply cut you off from solid nourishment and enjoyment – but also to see that the Lewis celebrated by evangelical devotees and looked down on by right-thinking Christian intellectuals was by no means the whole story. Rather like Thomas Merton (some of whose work Lewis read with appreciation),[3] Lewis was not always well served by the passion to publish every single word he ever wrote and to surround all those words with a glow of equal authority. But the immense industry of Lewis publication has at least meant that – especially through the monumental achievement of Walter Hooper in editing the letters – we have all the materials for a three-dimensional portrait.[4] This material helps us connect the man Lewis with the writer who so insistently scraped away at uncovering the varieties of self-delusion; who thus, you could say, gave us the tools with which we can question even some of his own positions. And to say this is one of the most serious compliments that could be paid to any thinker, a far more serious compliment than to assume that he or she is always right or wise.

That being said, I can only confess to being repeatedly humbled and reconverted by Lewis in a way that is true of few other modern Christian writers. Re-reading works I have not looked at for some time, I realize where a good many favourite themes and insights came from, and am constantly struck by the richness of imagination and penetration that can be contained even in a relatively brief letter. He is someone that you do not quickly come to the end of – as a complex personality and as a writer and thinker. In this brief study, I have wanted simply to display some of what has mattered most to me as a reader of Lewis over more than half a century.

What follows represents an expanded version of three lectures given in Canterbury Cathedral during Holy Week 2011, and I am very grateful to all those who attended, especially those who asked questions – and so prompted some further clarifications which have (I hope) found their way into this text. Particular thanks go to Sarah Goodall for her work in so efficiently and accurately transcribing these lectures from the recording.

For convenience, I have referred in the text to the omnibus edition of the Narnia books, *The Chronicles of Narnia* (London, HarperCollins, 2010). This arranges the books in 'chronological' order – i.e. beginning with *The Magician's Nephew*. Many, perhaps most, still prefer to read them in their order of publication – beginning with *The Lion, the Witch and the Wardrobe*. I have given not only page references to the one-volume edition, but also chapter references for those who are reading in other editions.

Also for convenience, and to reduce repetition, some of Lewis's book titles have been abbreviated: *The Lion, the Witch and the Wardrobe* (1950) is *The Lion*; *Prince Caspian* (1951) remains unabridged; *The Voyage of the Dawn Treader* (1952) is *Dawn Treader*; *The Silver Chair* (1953) is *Silver Chair*; *The Horse and His Boy* (1954) is *The Horse*; *The Magician's Nephew* (1955) is *Magician's Nephew*; and *The Last Battle* (1956) is *Last Battle*.

C. S. Lewis's Narnia books continue to captivate new generations of young readers, and I was delighted when my own children discovered them. This book is dedicated to my children, with memories of many hours spent reading aloud from Narnia and watching the new world open up for them.

Rowan Williams
Lambeth Palace, Easter 2012

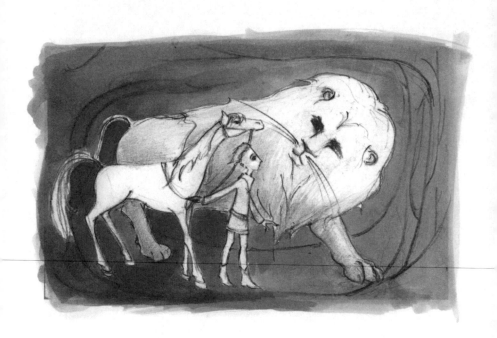

Introduction

Not every reader has been charmed by C. S. Lewis's Narnia stories, and the recent release of high-earning film versions of several of the books has renewed the controversy. Critics of Christian faith have been predictably vocal – though their comments often suggest at best a superficial reading of the books. But even among Christian readers, the reaction has not always been friendly. Notoriously, Lewis's friend, J. R. R. Tolkien, found them intolerable. He hated the random mixture of mythologies (classical Fauns and Dryads, Northern European giants and dwarfs, and, to add insult to injury, Father Christmas) and the failure, as he saw it, to create the kind of fully coherent imaginative world that he had spent his energies on for so long.

Not every reader has been charmed by C. S. Lewis's Narnia stories

Narnia is a very long way from Tolkien's Middle Earth. And Lewis seems to have had little or no interest in filling out the details in the way Tolkien – or Terry Pratchett – loves to do. He pays no attention to questions of what language his imagined people speak (Narnians and their neighbours in Calormen do not seem to need interpreters). He spends little time in elaborating details of culture or tradition (the Calormenes are taken over almost wholesale from the Arabian Nights, or so it seems at first; there are some qualifying factors, as we shall see). Very occasionally, as at the end of *The Horse*, there is reference to this or that episode of semi-legendary Narnian history, but these are casual moments. Lewis wants only to create a brief illusion of some extra dimension. And, as at least one reported conversation shows, he was blithely indifferent to breaches of internal consistency in the stories. His good friend, the poet Ruth Pitter, challenged him about how the Beaver family in *The Lion* manage to produce potatoes for their meal with the children, given the wintry conditions that had prevailed for most of living memory; not to mention oranges, sugar and suet for the marmalade roll . . .[1] Tolkien, one suspects, would have produced an appendix on the history and architecture of greenhouses in Narnia. But this is not Lewis's way. Some have impatiently concluded that he is not taking seriously enough the job of creating an alternative world – and thus of being too preoccupied with writing a piece of apologetic.

In fact, there has been quite a bit of discussion about how far he can be said to have had a plan for the whole sequence. Michael Ward's brilliant monograph[2] on the way in which

each book is coloured and shaped by the imagery asso-
ciated with a particular astrological sign – in a way very
typical of some kinds of mediaeval literature – has provided
not so much a structure for the interpretation of ideas in
the stories as an overall key to their symbolism and to what
might be called the 'flavour' of each book. Whatever exactly
Lewis intended when he wrote *The Lion*, it seems pretty
clear that the completed sequence does carry some of the
marks of a pattern such as Ward proposes. But it remains
very uncertain whether Lewis meant to write a whole series
from the start. In a letter to a young reader in 1957,[3] he
discusses the order in which the stories should be read (he
is inclined to prefer that they should be tackled in chronological order, i.e. beginning with *Magician's Nephew*), and
denies that he had a series in mind when writing *The Lion*.
Again, in 1959 he wrote to a schoolgirl, Sophia Storr, that
he had not initially envisaged what Aslan was going to 'do
and suffer' in *The Lion*.[4]

What he says here does underline that he is not in fact
casting around for a set of disconnected symbols to carry
a piece of concealed religious doctrine but allowing his
characters to emerge in the course of the story itself
and according to its logic. To try and map the entire set of
stories on to a single theological grid is difficult. As I hope

to show, there is a strong, coherent spiritual and theological vision shaping all the stories; but this does not necessarily

> There is a strong, coherent spiritual and theological vision shaping all the stories

mean that they must all be read as self-conscious allegories of theological truths. In the letter just mentioned, Lewis repudiates the idea of reading the stories as allegory and instead suggests that they answer the question of what sort of Incarnation and redemption would be appropriate in a world like Narnia.[5] So of course *The Lion* is 'about' the redemption of humankind at one level, a vivid reworking in terms of another, imagined world of one of the more dramatic theories of the atonement. But even here, the *story* has a logic that does not depend on having to fit in with a theological agenda. It could be – and regularly is – read by people who have no notion of such an agenda.

There are undoubtedly a few theologically taxing moments for a reader inclined to ask tiresome questions. If Aslan is the king of Narnia and 'the son of the great Emperor-beyond-the-Sea' (*The Lion* Ch. 8, p. 146), how exactly has his rule been superseded by that of the White Witch? If Aslan and the emperor are images of the divine Son and the divine Father, what has happened to the Holy Spirit (a question which, admittedly, can be asked of rather a lot of Western

Christian theology)? What are we to make of the beautiful passage in *The Horse* Chapter 11 where Aslan replies to Shasta's question, 'Who *are* you?' by repeating three times 'Myself' –

> very deep and low so that the earth shook: and again, 'Myself', loud and clear and gay; and then the third time, 'Myself', whispered so softly you could hardly hear it, and yet it seemed to come from all around you as if the leaves rustled with it.
>
> (p. 281)

This *sounds* as though Aslan is the Trinity, rather than just the Second Person of the Trinity; though a sympathetic theologian might be able to argue that the 'self' of any divine person has to be expressed always in terms of all three (Lewis mentions this passage as deliberately Trinitarian in his 1959 letter to Sophia Storr, but does not cast much light on how exactly we should read it).

We do Lewis no favours by pressing too hard on issues like this. The books must stand or fall, finally, as *stories*, and in what follows I have tried to take for granted that the theological insight will emerge from the narrative and the interaction of its characters, not from

> *The books must stand or fall, finally, as* stories

concentrating on what traditional theological themes might be encoded in this or that detail – though there are a fair few instances. Similarly, although there are a number of allusions to biblical stories or images, I have underlined only those that seem to me specially significant for a fuller understanding of what is going on.

Lewis has also been challenged on his doctrine of the Last Things, especially on his apparent 'liberalism' over the salvation of non-Christians. But here again, he should, I believe, be judged by the narrative force of what he has to say, particularly in *Last Battle*. If any reader of the books ends up feeling that the all-important and decisive role of Aslan is compromised by Lewis's narrative of how all are given the chance to see Aslan in the face and decide for or against him on the basis of what they most deeply desire and who they have made themselves to be, they are reading woodenly and artificially. Indeed, what Lewis implies in the way he deals with such questions is that some matters are better dealt with through narrative and imagination than through attempts at systematizing; a conclusion that shouldn't surprise any reader of Holy Scripture.

As I have said, I am not out to decode images or to uncover a system; but I do hope to show how certain central themes hang together – a concern to do justice to the *difference* of God, the disturbing and exhilarating otherness of what we encounter in the life of faith; a relentless insistence on self-questioning, not so as to understand ourselves in the abstract or as 'interesting' individuals, but simply to discover where we are afraid of the truth and where we turn away into self-serving falsehood; a passion to communicate the excess of joy that is promised by the truth of God in Christ. And, as I explain further in the first chapter, I want to capture something of what Lewis is trying to do in communicating – to a world that frequently thinks it knows what faith is – the character, the *feel*, of a real experience of surrender in the face of absolute incarnate love. Because that is what matters most: the possibility Lewis still offers of coming across the Christian story as if for the first time. Whether for the jaded believer or the contented unbeliever, the surprise of this joy is worth tasting.

1

The point of Narnia

A middle-aged bachelor teaching English Literature at Oxford proposes to publish a children's fantasy: in most publishers' offices, it is a proposal destined for the wastepaper basket. Yet no one could deny the extraordinary and continuing appeal of the Narnia stories – to adults as well as children. The enormous recent success of the series of films based on the books testifies to this. And even the ferocity of some critics of the books (about which there will be more to be said later) bears witness to their influence. Philip Pullman's powerful trilogy, *His Dark Materials*, is confessedly part of a counter-campaign[1] – as if recognizing that, for once, God has the best tunes and the devil (or rather the world of strictly secular morality and aspiration) needs to catch up in imaginative terms.

Why the books go on working so effectively is no easy question to answer. As I said in the Introduction, it isn't every reader, even every Christian reader, who finds them instantly compelling. Yet they bear many re-readings, and constantly disclose more things to think about. In this brief guide to some of their themes, I don't intend to try and answer the question of why they are popular – though there are some obvious things to be said. I am more interested in what precisely C. S. Lewis thought he was doing in writing the books in the first place.

Escape from adulthood?

The question of what Lewis thought he was doing is not quite the same question as 'What *prompted* him to write?' On this, there are various theories. Some biographers, including A. N. Wilson in his brilliant and contentious study of 1990, have made much of the fact that Lewis began work on *The Lion* at a time in his life when multiple stresses, personal and intellectual, were driving him back towards a long-lost world of childhood imagination where matters did not have to be settled by constant conflict. He had been much taken aback by a rather traumatic debate in Oxford with the formidable philosopher Elizabeth Anscombe, who had severely trounced him in argument, exposing major flaws in his book on miracles. Is it wholly an accident that the Narnia books have such a quota of terrifying female figures assaulting the simplicities of faith, hope and love?

And is Lewis retreating from argument back into the world of myth and fairy-tale which meant so much to him as a child? More damagingly, John Goldthwaite (to whose critique we shall be returning) claims that the Anscombe debate 'stung him back into the brooding of adolescence rather than the innocence of childhood', generating a fantasy picture of noble martyrdom at the hands of evil that finds its expression in Aslan's slaughter by the Witch.[2]

Lewis gives a little colour to such an explanation when he says both that he was writing the sort of books he himself would have liked to read and that he felt an urgent *need* to write them.[3] But the theory of an origin in some sort of panicked retreat from debate is pretty doubtful. Apart from the oddity of imagining Elizabeth Anscombe as the White Witch or the Queen of Underland (she was a passionately devout Roman Catholic who wanted simply to avoid the slightest suggestion that the faith was being defended by faulty reasoning),[4] it is an odd reading of the books that sees them as being in flight back to the simplicities of the nursery. They are successful children's books – but, like

Like most truly successful children's books, they are very far from just being comforting

most truly successful children's books, they are very far from just being comforting. Lewis wrote of *The Lion*, when early sales were slow, that some mothers and schoolteachers 'have decided that it is likely to frighten children', and then added wryly, 'I think it frightens adults, but v. few children'.[5] If these were indeed the kind of stories that Lewis felt he would like to read, it does credit to his appetite for challenge in his reading material. And in response to the notion that he is indulging in adolescent self-glorifying, we need to read all that is said again and again in the books about the dangers precisely of such melodrama – as I hope this chapter will show.

But it is also important to recognize how much the themes of the Narnia books are interwoven with what he was thinking and writing in other contexts around the same time, and with material he had already published in the 1940s – as well as the fact that the first seeds of the actual Narnia narrative seem to have been sown as early as 1939.[6] For example: his 1946 book, *The Great Divorce*, foreshadows many of the ideas in the Narnia stories – most particularly a theme that Lewis insists on more and more as his work develops, the impossibility of forcing any person to accept love and the monumental and excruciating difficulty of receiving love when you are wedded to a certain picture of yourself. It is this theme that emerges most clearly in his last (and greatest) imaginative work, the 1956 novel,

Till We Have Faces. The issues we shall be looking at in the following pages are very much the issues that Lewis is trying to work out in a variety of imaginative idioms from the early 1940s onwards – the problems of self-deception above all, the lure of self-dramatizing, the pain and challenge of encounter with divine truthfulness. What Narnia seeks to do, very ambitiously, is to translate these into terms that children can understand. And as to why Lewis decided to address such an audience, there is probably no very decisive answer except that he had a high view of children's literature, a passion for myth and fantasy and a plain desire to communicate as widely as possible.

In a letter of 1945 to Dorothy L. Sayers,[7] he declares that he is 'all for little books on other subjects with their Christianity latent. I propounded this in the S. C. R. [Senior Common Room] at Campion Hall [the Jesuit House of Studies in Oxford] and was told that it was "Jesuitical".' Against such a background, writing children's books 'with their Christianity latent' makes good sense enough. It is, we need to be clear, something rather different from simply writing standard defences of Christianity in code: he and Sayers would have agreed passionately that the writing has to have its own integrity, its own wholeness. It has to follow its own logic rather than being dictated by an argument. But this does not mean that it cannot be powerful in showing how an argument can be properly put into context. And if we turn back to his autobiography, *Surprised by Joy*, we shall find that this Jesuitical lack of scruple is simply a reflection of God's unprincipled methods in nudging us towards faith. 'A young man who wishes to remain a sound Atheist cannot be too careful of his reading,' says Lewis; apparently harmless literary works are littered with traps for the unwary, seductive style, compelling narrative and literary integrity blinding us to the doctrine that a writer takes for granted and so insinuating the doctrine when we're not paying full attention.[8]

The strangeness of God

So if we put aside the question of what exactly the *events* might have been that prompted the writing, can we now say something about what he is trying to do here? Perhaps the simplest way of answering the question is to say that Lewis is trying to recreate for the reader what it is *like* to encounter and believe in God. We are most of us still vaguely aware of language about God and Jesus in our society; alarmist

> *Lewis is trying to recreate for the reader what it is like to encounter and believe in God*

stories surface every year about how few schoolchildren can tell you what is supposed to have happened at the first Christmas or Easter, but there remains a general cultural memory of the Christian religion. Sharing the good news is not so much a matter of telling people what they have never heard as of persuading them that there are things they haven't heard when they think they *have*. Lewis repeatedly found, as did Dorothy Sayers, that they were dealing with a public who thought they knew what it was they were disbelieving when they announced their disbelief in Christian doctrine. The same situation is even more common today. It is not true that large numbers of people *reject* Christian faith – if by 'reject' we mean that they deliberately consider and then decide against it. They are imperceptibly shunted towards a position where the 'default setting' is a conviction that traditional Christianity has nothing much to be said for it. People who have settled down in this position are not likely to be much moved by argument; they need to be surprised into a realization that they have never actually reckoned with what Christianity is about.

Dorothy Sayers' letters of the early 1940s, when she was writing her radio plays on the life of Christ,[9] come back repeatedly to this point, and Lewis had already begun to explore the communication of the faith through fiction in his 'science fiction' trilogy, of which the first book was published as early as 1938. The first two deal, in various ways, with what the 'fallen' character of human action looks and feels like in an extraterrestrial context where there has never been what we understand by a fall – in worlds where certain kinds of natural attunement to the reality of the divine have never been lost. We are invited to see humanity as the tragic exception in a universe of intelligent beings – not as the destiny-bearers whose fearless exploratory courage will liberate all possible worlds. Humans let loose on other galactic civilizations are in fact toxic influences, and their colonizing and dominating ambitions are readily laid bare (Lewis had some very specific targets in mind among both popular scientific celebrities and writers of science fiction).

And the third of the trilogy, *That Hideous Strength* (1945), brings the action back to earth with (literally) a vengeance. It centres upon the fate of a young couple who have no serious spiritual roots and whose expectations of 'religion' are minimal and boring; what happens is that they are brought up directly against what it is that 'religion' is about – the real peril of damnation: that is, human souls radically and lastingly losing the possibility of good or well-being, but also the real possibility of joy beyond imagining, the fact that the world we think we know is soaked through with symbolic meaning and intelligent energy. And *that* is what Lewis is after in the Narnia books. He wants his readers to experience what it is that religious (specifically Christian) talk is about, without resorting to religious talk as we usually meet it.

> *The world we think we know is soaked through with symbolic meaning and intelligent energy*

How do you make fresh what is thought to be familiar, so familiar that it doesn't need to be thought about? Try making up a world in which these things can be met without preconceptions, a world in which the strangeness of the Christian story is encountered for what it is, not as part of a familiar eccentricity of behaviour called religion. Narnia is a strange place: a parallel universe, if you like. There is no 'church' in Narnia, no *religion* even. The interaction between Aslan as a 'divine' figure and the inhabitants of this world is something that is worked out in the routines of life itself. Indeed, the only organized religion in this world is the cult of Tash, the god of the Calormenes, a diabolical idol. A sharp-eyed reader will soon realize that 'Narnia' is both a name for the whole of this world and the name of one particular kingdom within it. But this is not careless writing: the kingdom of Narnia is where the action of Aslan is most clearly present and recognized, where the decisive things happen that shape the destiny of the rest of this world. And this means that the kingdom of Narnia is itself the 'Church', the community where transforming relation with Aslan becomes fully possible.

This is just one example of how Lewis makes fresh and strange the familiar themes of Christian doctrine. The realm of Narnia is a 'holy nation', to use the biblical term for Israel and the Church: it is the community in relation to which every human being's destiny is focused and determined, whether they realize it or not. To present this without creating in the parallel universe a parallel religious institution is a remarkable achievement.

Humanity in its place

There is another extremely important aspect of the realm of Narnia which picks up one of the themes of the science fiction trilogy in a new way: Narnia, unlike its immediate neighbours, is inhabited by talking animals, who are clearly shown as companions, in some sense equals, in the service of Aslan. Just as in the science fiction stories, especially the first, we are made to see humanity in a fresh perspective; the 'natural' pride or arrogance of the human spirit is chastened by the revelation that, in Narnia, you may be on precisely the same spiritual level as a badger or a mouse. Narnia is thus not only about encountering God in a new way; it is about thinking of your own humanity in a rich and surprising context. The 'holy nation' includes those whom we

In Narnia, you may be on precisely the same spiritual level as a badger or a mouse

think of as outside the all-important human story. But, as in the alien planets of the earlier trilogy, it is crucial to be able to look on humanity as, at best, part of a wider story, always in need of help from those with whom the planet is shared, and, at worst, a positively toxic presence, dragging its neighbours downwards. Lewis would have had plenty of questions to ask of fashionable environmentalism, but he sketches out with great prescience just the set of issues that more recent thinkers have brought into focus about the effects of certain conceptions of human uniqueness.

Anyone who imagines that Lewis does no more in his theology overall than reproduce what is popularly and wrongly supposed to be the 'Christian' attitude to the non-human Creation has to reckon with this. Leaving aside for the moment the deep roots that Lewis's actual view has in Christian tradition, it is absolutely clear that he wants to present humanity as occupying what you could call a focal but ambiguous place in Creation. There is no narrow focus on humanity at the expense of everything else. The presence of talking beasts means that the moral world is not exclusively human and that obligations and relationships are not restricted to intra-human affairs. Peter, towards the end of *The Lion* (Ch. 14, p. 754) addresses the talking dogs as 'cousins'; and we have got used in the course of *Last Battle* to the friendship between King Tirian and Jewel the unicorn.

Even more to the point, though, is the easily overlooked fact that humans themselves are initially aliens in Narnia. As *Magician's Nephew* makes plain, Narnia is designed for talking beasts: the intrusion first of Jadis and then of the various humans from our world who enter it is an accident resulting from Digory's foolishness in releasing Jadis from her magical slumbers in Charn. In the event, Aslan is able (of course) to turn this accident to profit by making the London cabby Frank and his wife Helen king and queen of Narnia. Humanity is a highly dangerous element in Creation, but it also has the capacity to protect and to guarantee justice. Frank is exhorted by Aslan to treat his animal subjects as free and intelligent, on the same footing as his own human descendants, but he still has an ultimate responsibility for them all.

The most eloquent statement of this double-edged character to human presence in the world is to be found in *Prince*

Caspian Chapter 15 (p. 416). Prince Caspian has just discovered that his people are descended from a tribe of pirates
(who, like so many other familiar figures in the books, have
come by accident into the world of Narnia); and he wishes
that he 'came of a more honourable lineage'.

> 'You come of the Lord Adam and the Lady Eve,' said Aslan.
> 'And that is both honour enough to erect the head of the
> poorest beggar, and shame enough to bow the shoulders of
> the greatest emperor on earth. Be content.'

There could not be a clearer depiction of the dual sense of
human dignity and human degradation that is central to the
orthodox Christian tradition. Lewis is simultaneously puncturing a glib humanist confidence in natural perfectibility and
protesting against any kind of metaphysical contempt for the
actual flesh and blood humanity around us. As *That Hideous
Strength* suggests, there can be a paradoxical fusion between
these two things. The search for social and individual perfection can lead to an angry impatience with 'ordinary' humanity,
even with the very processes of physical life. Humanity can
be manipulated into a nightmare caricature of eternal life,
but only by losing what makes it human. It is one of Lewis's
most durable and challenging insights.

Hence the importance of the animal world in Narnia.
Humans have to relate to animals as partners and equals –

equals in intelligence and dignity, even if in some sense they are to be governed by humans. Animals, even the smallest, play a central role in the stories, from the mice who nibble through the dead Aslan's bonds in *The Lion* Chapter 15 to the mice who feed the captive Tirian in *Last Battle* Chapter 4. Trufflehunter the badger in *Prince Caspian* and Reepicheep the mouse in *Prince Caspian* and *Dawn Treader* are not only major agents in the drama; they can act as a moral touchstone for humans, their virtues and their flaws acting as a somewhat exaggerated mirror to human habits. Behind this lies a long history of folk-tales and fairy-tales the world over which introduce 'animal helpers' in the quests of heroes, ranging from faithful and noble horses to magical counsellors (the Russian Firebird) to humble mice or dogs who ease the hero's path or save him from trouble (Hans Christian Andersen's 'Tinder-Box'). The sense that Lewis wants to convey is of a world in which humans are not alone as intelligent actors, actors in a theatre of providential and theologically meaningful events.

Some varieties of impoverished and nervous modern Christian mind have been anxious about this, as about Lewis's blithe co-options of pagan mythology (Dryads and so on, not to mention the astrological subtexts whose presence is hard to deny).[10] But for Lewis the crucial theological point about the key role of human beings in the moral cosmos is only intelligible when we see that human beings are always already embedded in their relations with the non-human world and that their moral quality is utterly bound up with this as much as with their mutual relations. To be invited to see trees and rivers as part of the 'people' of Narnia, and to have to ask what proper and respectful relations might be between a human and a talking beast is to be jolted out of a one-dimensional understanding of human uniqueness or human destiny under God. To be human is to be *with* the non-human world, even to be *for* the non-human world.

> To be human is to be with the non-human world, even to be for the non-human world

Of course there are areas of strain in this picture. Lewis, as we have noted, thinks vegetarians are silly; his favoured characters are all unapologetic carnivores. But this creates a bit of a difficulty with talking beasts. When Puddleglum discovers in the giants' stronghold (*Silver Chair* Ch. 9) that he has inadvertently eaten a talking stag, he is sickened. It is quite clear that eating talking beasts is strictly taboo, for the obvious reason that humans make real, lasting and mutual relationships with these beasts. But as for the rest? Is it quite enough to make an easy distinction between the two classes of animal, one capable of intelligent relationship, the other created for labour and fodder? Lewis makes no attempt to resolve this except in the Creation scenes in *Magician's Nephew* (Ch. 9, p. 69), where Aslan picks out pairs of animals from among their peers to endow them with reason and speech. There is a tension here between the assertions, implicit and explicit, of the significance of bodily life in its natural integrity and a sort of arbitrary gulf between beasts of the same physical nature who have different 'mental' or even spiritual qualities; as if the fact that some animals have something like human dignity is *conditional* on their having a certain set of mental qualities. Press this too far and you end up creating difficulties for the idea of human dignity itself.

But we have to recognize that, like many others, Lewis would have found no ultimate incompatibility in professing a deep respect for the animal Creation at the same time as regarding it as being there to serve human needs, in at least some regards. His talking beasts introduce an insoluble moral complication to this fairly simple picture. But, as we have seen, he is not too concerned to produce a wholly self-consistent world. His didactic point is still a powerful one: what if you found yourself obliged to make *conversation* with non-human partners? To make friends with them? Start from here and you may find that it changes your attitude to the world around you in radical ways. At the very least, it may save you from the passionate campaign against nature itself that is typical of the most toxic kinds of modernity.

And above all, the ruler and saviour of Narnia is not human. Here too it is probably not a good idea to press for too much consistency. Lewis captures a great many fundamental theological ideas in the figure of Aslan; but the one that, in the nature of the case, he cannot bring in is that of the saviour who restores the divine image in human life, who 'reconstructs' the humanity that has been lost by selfishness and stupidity. But if – a substantial if – we could think about the life of the saviour, even the suffering of the saviour, without thinking of his solidarity with us, might we learn something? I don't for a moment think that Lewis would have argued that this theme of solidarity is secondary or dispensable to Christian doctrine. But, in spite of everything, he is not *just* trying to 'translate' Christian doctrine; he is trying to evoke what it feels like to believe in the God of Christian revelation, and his portrayal of Aslan is an extremely daring essay in bringing to the foreground what is obscured by a too habitual and too easy stress on solidarity.

Aslan's strangeness and wildness, as we have seen, are powerfully conveyed by his animal character. And the idea that we are saved by what we should otherwise be tempted to think of as 'beneath' us in the order of Creation can be read as really just an intensified version of the orthodox theological point that the saviour stoops to the lowest of conditions, and that we must stoop to meet him. In other words, part of what is involved in accepting what Aslan offers is accepting liberation and authority at the hands of an agent who is strange, even (apparently) badly equipped to offer such things. And this is in itself a more than respectable biblical theme. 'Is not this the carpenter's son?' – the question sceptically asked by Jesus' fellow-townsmen – is just about recognizably in the same territory as 'Is not this a being of inferior status?'

Lewis once referred to certain kinds of book as a 'mouthwash for the imagination.'[11] This is what he attempted to provide in the Narnia stories: an unfamiliar world in which we could rediscover what it might mean to meet the holy without the staleness of religious preconceptions as they appear in our culture. The point of Narnia is to help us rinse out what is stale in our thinking about Christianity – which is almost everything. There are of course many fine strands of hint and allusion that connect us back to the language

The point of Narnia is to help us rinse out what is stale in our thinking about Christianity

we know, and we shall be noting a few of them as we move on. But the essential thing is this invitation to hear the story as if we had never heard it before. And for a growing number of readers who actually *haven't*, the effectiveness can be measured.

2

Narnia and its critics

I mentioned earlier the way in which Philip Pullman had conceived his own trilogy as a sort of riposte to the Narnia books. The parallels are clear enough – an alternative universe including talking animals, even (though Pullman might dispute this) an active and independent heroine, if we give due weight to how Lucy is portrayed in *The Lion*. And it is possible to see how Pullman's aims correspond to Lewis's as we have just explained them. Pullman's parallel world is one in which we encounter God in a way that strips away the conventions that in our world conceal his real nature – only, in Pullman, that 'real nature' is a fiction. It is something projected by those who want arbitrary power, a great fantasy that sanctions systematic abuse, oppression and corruption. The God of these stories is 'objectively' no more than a self-deluded angel, now senile and helpless, but allowed to survive because he is the symbolic focus and rationale for unaccountable human authority.

Pullman has been eloquent in his denunciation of the ethics of Narnia[1] but he has not been alone in this; even J. K. Rowling, who has none of Pullman's ideological agenda, has expressed her reservations, and John Goldthwaite in a book already referred to, *The Natural History of Make-Believe*,[2] mounted an impassioned frontal assault on the sexism, violence and racial stereotyping of Lewis's narratives. It may be helpful to look briefly at these accusations, to assess their weight.

A writer of his time

The first thing to say – with boring obviousness – is that Lewis is a male writer of the 1950s, with more than his share of the prejudices and stereotypes of his period. But even more, he is often very deliberately recreating the atmosphere of the Victorian and Edwardian children's books he had enjoyed as a child himself. F. Anstey, E. Nesbit, Kenneth Grahame and others haunt his style and his images – Nesbit perhaps above all. There is a Nesbit story involving a magic wardrobe; and Queen Jadis's visit to London in *Magician's Nephew* is shamelessly cribbed from the riotous episode in Nesbit's *The Story of the Amulet* where the Queen of Babylon arrives in London as a result of a magical oversight and creates havoc – including (for those with an eye to the political content of children's books) a massacre in the Stock Exchange, magically reversed in due course but decidedly gory while it lasts, and with some very uncomfortable anti-Semitic prejudices just off-stage. A good many other incidents and ideas from Nesbit are reworked in Narnia. These Nesbit echoes explain why Lewis's children sound at times just a little old-fashioned even for the 1950s. And the scene-setting at the beginning of *Magician's Nephew* refers quite openly to Nesbit's books about the Bastables, whose adventures finally free them from the genteel poverty in which they live. In other words, the reader in the twenty-first century has to make allowance for nearly a hundred years of change.

> *The reader in the twenty-first century has to make allowance for nearly a hundred years of change*

There is, though, one feature of the Edwardian style which Lewis reproduces to great effect, a feature which rather tells against the simple conclusion that using this template drives him in an unbrokenly conservative direction. The best children's authors of that period, Nesbit above all, are expert in creating a sense of collusion between author and young reader at the expense of the adult world. The author will refer to familiar bits of received adult wisdom only to mock them: phrases like 'Grown-ups will tell you that . . .' or 'I expect you've heard people saying . . .' occur regularly, usually with the rider that you needn't believe all that adults say. And the effect is of a benign conspiracy between author and reader that gently undercuts conventional wisdom. It is part of the strategy that makes fantasy, or at least dramatic adventure, credible and acceptable. The reader is being told that in these pages the ordinary wisdom of the grown-up world is suspended; it is all right to indulge fantasy. It is both a quiet subversion (remember that a good many classic children's authors were radicals in their hopes for society) and a successful way of containing and making safe a set of fantasies that may be disturbing: the author is on your side. And of course Lewis brilliantly extends this in *The Lion* when the professor, faced with the counter claims of Lucy and Edward about the reality of Narnia, exposes the groundlessness of assuming that Edward must be right. Susan, who has been trying to respond in an 'adult' way, 'had never dreamed that a grown-up would talk like the professor and didn't know what to think' (*The Lion* Ch. 5, p. 131). But the fact is that the professor is talking like the authorial voice of an Edith Nesbit.

Narnia and the 'other'

That being said, the question of prejudice and stereotype will not go away. Some have made great play of the way in which the Calormenes (subliminally 'coloured men', as has been suggested?) are described – dark-skinned, cruel, clad in turbans and armed with scimitars, over-sophisticated and elaborate in speech, devotees of an alien and terrifying god. These are quite obviously aspects of what is usually called 'orientalism', the Western habit of depicting non-Western civilizations as exotic, decadent and sinister. The Calormenes talk like characters in the 'Arabian Nights', with an effect that can be both comic and threatening, and they are clearly the dangerous 'other' where Narnia is concerned. Some recent critics have argued that they represent the demonizing of Islam that continues to disfigure the Western imagination.

The accusation about Islam can be put by fairly easily. As several have noted, the religion of the Calormenes is polytheistic and involves images and human sacrifice. It may be a reflection of 'orientalist' pictures of Asian (especially Indian) practice, but has no points of contact at all with Islam. But the problems come with two remaining areas where it is much harder to defend Lewis. The first is that, whether or not Islam is in view, the *cultural* world of the

Calormenes is unmistakably Arab, and their relation to Narnia is that of mediaeval 'Saracens' to Christendom as reflected in the literature of the period. The polarity of 'the West and the rest' is unavoidable in such a representation (it is worth observing in passing that this is by no means wholly absent from Pullman's work, where 'Turks' and 'Tartars' appear as stereotypical villains); the shadow of the Crusades is much in evidence. As Goldthwaite notes, when Shasta in

The Horse first encounters Narnians, he sees them as somehow 'nicer' and more 'normal' than the Calormenes (*The Horse* Ch. 4, p. 231); quite apart

> **The shadow of the Crusades is much in evidence**

from the implausibility of this, it unquestionably sets up a picture of (white) Narnians as intrinsically more attractive, kinder, less formal and inscrutable. It is an uncomfortable passage, to put it mildly. Certainly, it is unexceptional in a book of its time, but that does not make it more acceptable. The second is that Lewis undoubtedly shared some of the most unreconstructed ideas of his generation about Eastern religions – as comes through, for example, in a letter to his brother in 1932; and there is a rather odd passage about Hinduism towards the end of *Surprised by Joy*.[3] It is an area where his debt to G. K. Chesterton shows, as anyone will confirm who recalls the characterizations of 'Eastern' culture and religion that you find in the Father Brown stories, for instance. However, even in this regard Lewis's thinking did not remain static, as his letters to his former pupil Bede Griffiths indicate.[4] And at the very least, his pictures are less crude than the really offensive representations of Eastern religion and culture that have passed without much comment in – for example – the Indiana Jones films in more recent years.

As to the 'Arabian Nights' language, either the reader finds this funny or s/he does not. It is, remember, less a parody of Arab or Oriental speech than a comic version of the stilted way in which Oriental speech was usually translated into English, a laboured blend of the biblical and the mediaeval. You could compare it with Ernest Bramah's Kai Lung stories, which create a comic pastiche of Chinese speech as rendered by English translators. When, in *The Horse*, we meet the Calormene ruler, his son and the Grand Vizier and listen to their exchanges, we may recognize that the parody is broad; but it is not just demeaning or mocking:

> 'How well it was said by a gifted poet,' observed the Vizier, raising his face (in a somewhat dusty condition) from the carpet, 'that deep draughts from the fountain of reason are desirable in order to extinguish the fire of youthful love.'

This seemed to exasperate the Prince. 'Dog,' he shouted, directing a series of well-aimed kicks at the hindquarters of the Vizier . . .

The Tisroc was apparently sunk in thought, but when, after a long pause, he noticed what was happening, he said tranquilly:

'My son, by all means desist from kicking the venerable and enlightened Vizier: for as a costly jewel retains its value even if hidden in a dung-hill, so old age and discretion are to be respected even in the vile persons of our subjects.'

(*The Horse* Ch. 8, pp. 256–7)

Lewis cannot by any means be wholly acquitted of the racial and cultural prejudices of his day; and he does not have to be beyond fault to be admired or loved, any more than any other serious writer. But we shall not understand what he is doing unless we read him mindful of the tradition of storytelling he is both continuing and parodying.

Female characters

The charges of sexism or misogyny, though, are harder to counter. Even a very sympathetic commentator like Stella Gibbons (author of *Cold Comfort Farm* and a rather unexpected admirer of Lewis) complains that Lewis disliked 'women who have entered rather boldly into the world that men have reserved for themselves. The domesticated, fussy, kind woman gets an occasional pat on her little head – (Mrs Beaver in *The Lion*, Ivy Maggs in *That Hideous Strength*).'[5] Much feeling has been generated by the banishment of Susan from *Last Battle* because 'She's interested in nothing nowadays except nylons and lipstick and invitations. She was always a jolly sight too keen on being grown-up' (*Last Battle* Ch. 12, p. 741). Susan has forgotten Narnia apparently with the onset of puberty, and this has led some to conclude that she is 'damned' for reaching sexual maturity.

This is unfair. We have already met (in *The Horse*) a mature *Narnian* Susan, courted by the heir to the Calormene throne. Her failure is not growing up. It is the denial of what she has known, rooted in her 'keenness' not to grow up but to *be* grown-up, a very different matter. 'It is the stupidest children who are most childish and the stupidest grown-ups who are most grown-up,' we are told in Chapter 16 of *The Silver Chair* (p. 661). Susan is guilty of what Edmund in *The Lion* is initially guilty of, no more and no less, which is the refusal to admit the reality of Narnia when you have actually lived there. In *The Lion* this denial is one of the things that open the door to Edmund's more serious treachery (so it is hardly a gender-specific matter); the issue is precisely that truthfulness which again and again – as we shall see – emerges as the central moral focus of the Narnia stories. And of course Susan's longer-term future as an adult in 'our' world is left entirely open. Lewis himself wrote in 1960 to a young reader distressed by Susan's defection that he was reluctant to write the story of Susan's rediscovery of Narnia.

> Not that I have no hope of Susan's ever getting to Aslan's country, but because I have a feeling that the story of her journey would be longer and more like a grown-up novel than I wanted to write. But I may be mistaken. Why not try it yourself?[6]

Nor does Lewis in fact give us a series of weak or ill-defined female characters. Lucy's courage and determination are a constant theme in the books where she appears. In *Prince Caspian*, when Edmund says 'to Peter and the Dwarf' that girls 'can never carry a map in their heads', it is Lucy who retorts 'That's because our heads have got something inside them' (*Prince Caspian* Ch. 9, p. 370) and ends the conversation. In *Dawn Treader* Chapter 8, Lucy again castigates her male companions for being such 'swaggering, bullying idiots' when Edmund and Caspian quarrel over who will be overlord of the island where water magically turns things to gold (p. 484). Aravis in *The Horse* is as forceful and intelligent a figure as any. It is true enough that Lewis seems to be all too ready to deal with the extremes of the spectrum where female characters are concerned – witch-queens and nannies. But in between there is rather more than some readers have noticed of ordinary female intelligence; and the depiction of male jostling for position among both boys and men, and the lethal consequences of this male pride, is none too flattering. It will not do to see Lewis as a simple misogynist. It is tempting to say that the further he gets away from *theorizing* about gender characteristics, the better he is in depicting women; the problem with

> *It will not do to see Lewis as a simple misogynist*

the ill-starred Jane in *That Hideous Strength* is – as Stella Gibbons once again observes – that she has to carry an uncomfortable weight of theory in the very complex plot of that strange work.[7]

Violent endings

Finally, violence. There have been objections to the glorifying of killing and physical force, Aslan instructing Peter to clean his sword after the battle in *The Lion*, a quite bloodily and realistically described battle in *The Horse* Chapter 13, the fight (under Aslan's direction) with the school bullies at the end of *Silver Chair*, and so on.

Lewis has contrived a Christ willing to turn his back while his chosen children, in the name of vengeance, beat up another group of children. We have seen this puppet Christ often enough before, marching at the head of innumerable armies and mobs.[8]

There is no denying that Lewis's narrative has the insouciant attitude to violent death that characterized a great deal of historical fiction for boys throughout most of his life. For a lot of the time, he inhabits quite uncritically the conventions of chivalric adventure, 'knightly' slaughter of the wicked. And the ending of *Silver Chair* is indeed painfully weak: the facile satire directed against progressive education is too obviously Lewis indulging in partisan grumbling, and the trouncing of the bullies is a forced and blustering bit of school-story cliché.

But yet again we cannot simply say that he is uncritical about violence. In *Last Battle* Chapters 2 and 3, King Tirian and Jewel the unicorn attack and kill a group of Calormene slave-drivers who are ill-treating a group of talking animals, and then feel deeply ashamed. They have killed unarmed men, and, for all that there is provocation, there is no glory about it. It will not do to claim that Lewis is, in any of the passages that have caused such offence, simply giving a blanket justification for violence against unbelievers. And the idea that he somehow sanctions the coercion of the mob, in any form, is a seriously perverse reading. As Stanley Hauerwas has observed in an impressively careful discussion of Lewis on violence and war,[9] he identifies many of the weaknesses of popular pacifism with great insight; but he also shows signs of at least imagining what is the essence of the non-violent stance, the patience to leave outcomes in the hands of God when other resource is exhausted. And he was quite clear – with due respect to Goldthwaite's polemic – that *at best* the chivalric impulse is a stage along the road that may finally lead us to understand martyrdom.

We shall come back later to the larger question of how death is handled in the stories, but it may help to note at this point that Lewis had a deep-seated and robust conviction that death was not the worst thing that could happen to anyone. Whether the contemporary reader agrees or not, it is salutary to have to think through what this means and not resort too quickly to fastidious objections – oddly fastidious in a culture in which the imagery of violence in 'entertainment' for all ages is unprecedentedly gross. But that is another story.

In short, Lewis is indisputably a writer whose instinctive – and sometimes quite deliberate – attitudes to women and ethnic 'others' are abrasive for most contemporaries. But – as with any pre-modern writer – what is interesting is not how Lewis reflects the views of an era but how he qualifies or undercuts them in obedience to the demands of a narra-

> *What is interesting is not how Lewis reflects the views of an era but how he qualifies or undercuts them*

tive or a spiritual imperative or both (this is a good principle for reading Augustine or Aquinas or Calvin, or even Shakespeare . . .). We have seen some of how he does this; and we have seen hints already of the ways in which the stories are set up to disturb easy conclusions or conventional expectations. To come to the heart of this disturbance, we have to turn to the controlling figure in the whole sequence, the wild animal who rules the holy nation.

3

Not a tame lion

The Lion, the Witch and the Wardrobe carefully prepares the way for Aslan's appearance. When in Chapter 7 Mr Beaver confides 'in a low whisper' that 'They say Aslan is on the move' (p. 141), we are given a glimpse of what is instantly evoked by the name for the children. They do not know who Aslan is, 'any more than you do', as Lewis tells the reader, but 'some enormous meaning' is called up, like something heard or glimpsed in a dream that mysteriously promises to give shape to an otherwise chaotic bundle of events or impressions. Edmund feels horror, Peter feels 'brave and adventurous', Susan has the sensation of a scent or a strain of music, and Lucy 'got the feeling you have when you wake up in the morning and realize that it is the beginning of the holidays or the beginning of summer'.

It is not only that Aslan promises 'meaning' (and that, as Lewis doesn't let us forget, can be menacing for some): this meaning is something subversive, rebellious. This element in the Narnia stories has been rather overlooked. Aslan may

It is not only that Aslan promises 'meaning': this meaning is something subversive, rebellious

be the rightful king of Narnia, but he makes his first appearance as a rebel against the established order. Part of the emotion triggered by his name as the story works towards his appearance is to do with the overthrow of a tyrannical order. In *Prince Caspian* the elements of conspiracy and revolt are even more pronounced, and the story carries much the same emotional register as *The Lion*, with a similar explosion of liberating festivity at its conclusion. If we think back to what I suggested were Lewis's basic aims in the story, we can see that he is introducing us to a God who, so far from being the guarantor of the order that we see around us, is its deadly enemy.

Lewis tells us in his autobiography[1] of how he readily adopted in his schooldays the language of revolt against the tyranny of 'orthodoxy' and imposed order, with God as the representative of this tyranny. 'I maintained that God did not exist. I was also very angry with Him for not existing. I was equally angry with Him for creating a world.' He knew very well what it felt like to think about God as the power responsible for making a world of unavoidable suffering; and in *The Lion* he builds up a very different kind of picture with great skill. Tyranny and suffering and above all the dreary dictatorship of unthinking and bullying power are what Aslan delivers us from. Lewis's debt to G. K. Chesterton is a large one, and not the least of it is in this aspect of his storytelling. Chesterton's *The Man Who Was Thursday* is perhaps the most dramatic example of this technique of making orthodoxy sound like rebellion or even anarchy. As readers of that book will recall, the plot turns on the idea that keeping the law – indeed, maintaining the fabric of the universe itself – must have the character of adventure, even revolt, so that we do not forget the sheer surprisingness of the world we inhabit.

A disturbing presence

It is a consistent theme in Lewis. The truth of God is found in rebellion against the oppressive clichés of the world. It is, in a rather different mode, the theme of *The Screwtape Letters*: the perspective of the devils is a tidy and orderly one, so tidy and orderly that it successfully conceals the ultimate nonsense of the spiritual world they inhabit, whose goals can only be control or absorption of each

> The truth of God is found in rebellion against the oppressive clichés of the world

· 51 ·

other. Against this joyless order stands the unpredictable world of grace, which the devils cannot understand – another recurrent theme in Lewis, that evil is ultimately 'tone-deaf' to good, and thus always vulnerable to the divine surprise. In a well-known letter to Bede Griffiths in 1941, Lewis praises an undergraduate essay he has just read on Milton, quoting the student's description of the diabolical ideal in *Paradise Lost* as 'an ordered state of sin', which sounds deeply convincing until we notice that it means 'living to ourselves' and our consciences are startled.[2]

The orderliness of a world focused on the self is doomed to be disrupted by grace; and we can't appreciate quite what Aslan is about unless and until we see him in action against this kind of order. It is significant that in *That Hideous Strength* the young protagonist, Mark, is moved to rebellion against the sinister technocratic elite who are plotting world domination when he is required to stamp on a crucifix: he has no real idea what the crucifix represents, but he is dimly aware that Jesus 'had lived and been executed thus by the Belbury of those days' (Belbury being the headquarters of the conspirators). With no rationale that he can express, he revolts, in favour of whatever it is that is *not* the inhuman lust for order and control that he has up to this point found so seductive – knowing that there is no guarantee of being vindicated, for him any more than for the figure on the cross. 'If the universe was a cheat, was that a good reason for joining its side? . . . Why not go down with the ship?'[3]

In *Last Battle*, Shift, the ape who is trying to take over Narnia by manipulating false images and expectations of Aslan, gives himself away most decisively when he defines his hopes for the future of Narnia and quashes opposition. In the new Narnia, 'There'll be oranges and bananas pouring in – and roads and big cities and offices and whips and muzzles and saddles and cages and kennels and prisons – oh, everything.' When an old bear objects that they don't want these things because they want to be free, the ape explodes: 'You think freedom means doing what you like. Well, you're wrong. That isn't true freedom. True freedom means doing what I tell you' (Ch. 3, p. 685). The great philosophical historian Isaiah Berlin provided, in a very famous lecture, an analysis of the danger we face when freedom is defined as the liberty to do certain carefully specified things as identified by political philosophers; it is the same point that is made with economy and elegance in Lewis's portrayal of Shift.

It shouldn't surprise us, then, if Aslan's freedom is so often depicted as riotous – literally, at one point in *Prince Caspian*, 'bacchanalian', when the god Bacchus himself and even a drunken Silenus are brought on stage, as in the revels of classical Greece (this sort of thing makes some Christian – and other – readers of Narnia very nervous . . .).[4] In *The Lion* (Ch. 16), Aslan breathes life into stone as he restores to life those who have been petrified by the White Witch – among them the delightful Christmas party whose celebrations have so infuriated the Witch in Chapter 11. And Chapter 14 of *Prince Caspian* – disarmingly titled, 'How All were Very Busy' – depicts a liberation that extends from nature spirits to schoolchildren. A river god rises up to destroy a bridge, and two miserable schools are turned upside down by the arrival of Aslan (and Bacchus). One is 'a girls' school, where a lot of Narnian girls, with their hair done very tight and ugly tight collars round their necks and thick tickly stockings on their legs, were having a history lesson'. Gwendolen, rebuked for looking out of the window by Miss Prizzle, is swept up in the festive riot. '"You'll stay with us, sweetheart?" said Aslan. "Oh, *may* I? Thank you, thank you," said Gwendolen.' And an exhausted female teacher in a boys' school 'looked out of the window and saw the divine revellers singing up the street and a stab of joy went through her heart'. The boys are scattered (and turned into pigs, it would appear) by Bacchus, and '"Now, Dear Heart", said Aslan to the Mistress: and she jumped down and joined them' (pp. 408–9).

The 'ordered state of sin' clearly isn't just the tyranny of a White Witch or a King Miraz; it is whatever makes drab and oppressive the flow of joy and energy in the world of animals, humans – and even rivers. And there is also here another element that tends to be overlooked, one that is not easy to discuss sensibly. Aslan speaks, here as elsewhere, to those he meets in terms of strong endearments; for the adult reader, there is bound to be something very like an erotic charge to this intimacy. These are children's stories, so Lewis is content to leave it close to but not quite breaking the surface. But in *That Hideous Strength* we have a much more explicit hint in the same direction. Towards the end of the book, Jane, rather nervous and (in Lewis's eyes) over-intellectual, is conscripted into making up a bed for another couple, about to be reunited after a long time. Her attempts are foiled by the arrival of an overwhelming, rather barbaric female presence, accompanied by a crowd of manic gnomes who throw the bedclothes around in disorder and leave Jane frightened and disoriented. She is told by her friends that she has met the 'earthly Venus': her (irreligious) Puritanism has been confronted by raw eros, festive and disruptive.[5] Now the advent of 'Venus' is not the advent of an Aslan; but this breaking in to Jane's anxious and controlled world is quite clearly portrayed as part of her opening-up to grace. And it is unashamedly sexual.

As I have said, it is difficult to discuss this without giving a variety of false impressions. Lewis is not advancing an erotic mysticism; *That Hideous Strength* specifically registers this as a possibility at one point and turns away from it. He is not claiming that Aslan/Christ is to be met in erotic adventures. Nor is he giving any house room to the idea that encounter with Christ is a substitute for ordinary sexual enjoyment. This is an idea that he sees off in short order in a very forceful passage in *A Grief Observed.*[6] It would be better to say that what Lewis is trying to evoke is a world in which the profoundest physical enjoyment is one of the best and clearest images of what it is to meet God. That meeting is therefore never a *substitute* for physical fulfilment, nor is physical fulfilment a means to encounter with God. It is simply that erotic satisfaction fully enjoyed is one of the most powerful glimpses we can have of what union with God is like – a point entirely consonant with a great deal in the tradition of Christian contemplation. Remember that Lewis is constantly trying to get us to sense afresh what it is *like* to be confronted with

> The profoundest physical enjoyment is one of the best and clearest images of what it is to meet God

God. In the Narnia stories, he goes as far as he can towards this erotic realm without breaking the proper boundaries of a narrative for children.

He does it by making his 'divine' presence an *animal*. Aslan's physicality is capable of being explored and enjoyed by the children in the stories in something of the way a child explores and enjoys the presence of a large pet – though this way of putting it is to risk trivializing. Aslan's animality permits the evoking of physical pleasure without trespassing directly on the realm of adult erotic experience. So Susan and Lucy in *The Lion* Chapter 15 can roll on the ground with the resurrected Aslan ('whether it was more like playing with a thunderstorm or playing with a kitten Lucy could never make up her mind'; p. 185), and Aslan can give Caspian 'the wild kisses of a lion' at the end of *The Silver Chair* (Ch. 16, p. 661). It is a considerable risk in the storytelling, moving towards an awkward frontier; but as a solution to how you convey overwhelming physical enjoyment as a glimpse of the divine, it is – for most readers – remarkably successful.

The animality also underlines one of the major themes of the books. Animals may be more or less domesticated, but even playing with a kitten can produce a scratch or two. 'Is he – quite safe?' asks Susan in Chapter 7 of *The Lion*.

'Who said anything about safe? 'Course he isn't safe,' says Mr Beaver; 'But he's good.' Aslan's unsafeness is referred to repeatedly: 'Is it not said in all the old stories that He is not a Tame Lion?' (*Last Battle* Ch. 2, p. 677). But what is perhaps most remarkable in the entire sequence – and in itself a compelling reason for never reading the books without including *Last Battle* – is the way Lewis allows this very axiom almost to undermine faith and truth. To take a parallel from as different an author as you could imagine, Dostoevsky can write in his personal journals of how he has learned to sing his hosanna in the crucible of doubt – but he also, in *The Brothers Karamazov*, uses precisely this phrase in the mouth of a diabolical visitant as a mocking summary of religious evasiveness and dishonesty.[7] Similarly, when the malign Shift begins his campaign to take over Narnia, the fact that he orders things that are absolutely contrary to what might be expected of Aslan is initially met with confusion rather than rejection – because 'he's not a tame lion'. Is he bound by his own rules? There have been no signs in the stars to announce the coming again of Aslan; but 'he is not the slave of the stars but their Maker' (*Last Battle* Ch. 2, p. 677). Appealing to the unpredictable wildness of Aslan has become an unanswerable tool of control. When the talking animals question and protest at the ape's dictates, Shift replies, 'He isn't going to

be soft any more . . . He'll teach you to think he's a tame lion'
(*Last Battle* Ch. 3, p. 684).

Worse is to come, though. Once the language about Aslan's
wildness has become something the ape exploits for his
advantage, it is fatally compromised. King Tirian attempts
to explain to the dwarfs in Chapter 7 that the false Aslan
has been exposed, but finds that they are no longer able to
believe that there is a *true* Aslan. All language about Aslan
must be exploitative; 'We're not going to be fooled again.'
And Tirian makes the mistake of saying that he cannot
produce the true Aslan because 'he's not a tame lion'.

'The Dwarfs at once began repeating "not a tame lion, not
a tame lion" in a jeering sing-song. "That's what the other
lot kept telling us," said one' (p. 707).

You could say that the ultimate test of any religious or,
indeed, imaginative vision is to see if it can survive the most
uncompromisingly cynical, parodic hostile representation
of it; this is what Lewis is doing here, and it needs to be
taken very seriously. The utter corruption of the 'not a tame
lion' axiom; the recognition that Aslan does not appear
any longer ('What if the real Aslan turns up?' protests the
hapless donkey that Shift persuades to impersonate Aslan;
'He never does turn up,' the ape replies; *Last Battle* Ch. 2,
p. 674), the nightmare possibility that Aslan is not what he

has been believed to be ('As if the sun rose one day and were a black sun'; *Last Battle* Ch. 3, p. 682) – all of this is Lewis introducing, very boldly, something like the concept of the 'night of the spirit' into the reader's imagination. For the adult reader of Lewis, there is a haunting anticipation of the outbursts in *A Grief Observed* at a God who appears as a 'Cosmic Sadist', a vivisector.[8] *Last Battle*, certainly the most complex and in many ways the most uneven of the Narnia sequence, is also the one that pushes us closest to the edge of denial or refusal.

It is not, of course, the first time that we have been brought dangerously near the fire. Chapter 12 of *Silver Chair* shows us its heroes Eustace and Jill, with their wonderfully imagined companion, the compulsively gloomy Puddleglum, trapped in 'Underland' by its witch-queen, who is seeking to persuade them that they have never lived above ground, indeed, that the world above is a myth, a dream. The Lion is a fantasy produced by thinking of a bigger cat; the idea of a sun is the result of trying to imagine a bigger and better lamp. 'Put away these childish tricks' (Ch. 12, p. 632). The children are on the point of giving in; but Puddleglum resists. What if all the memory of the overworld *is* fantasy: isn't it strange that such a fantasy can appear so much richer than the sup- posedly real things, 'this black pit of a kingdom of yours'?

Puddleglum decides in favour of 'the play-world': 'I'm on Aslan's side even if there isn't any Aslan to lead it' (p. 633). And this declaration of utterly 'blind' faith is what prompts the Witch to reveal herself in her true colours, as a venomous serpent.

This is not quite the emotional darkness of *Last Battle*, but it prepares us for it by inviting us to imagine a world in which the heart of the story is being written off as nonsense. Puddleglum's refusal to turn his back on Aslan even if Aslan is a fiction is another bold moment. Lewis is by no means giving ground to the idea that the truth of religious language doesn't matter as it is a question of will and commitment only – a position not unfamiliar in twentieth-century philosophy of religion. But he does allow himself to think of what it is like to have to choose between a world that, while 'reasonable', is actually smaller than what we experience and a world whose reality we cannot establish but which offers firmer ground to stand on. Again, we are not a million miles from Dostoevsky: his notorious assertion that, faced with the choice between Christ and the truth, he would choose Christ has caused much controversy,[9] but he is surely saying something close to what Lewis is after here. If the price of some kinds of even well-attested 'truth' is the abolition of some dimensions of human imagining, it is too high. And,

in certain moods, the most dedicated believer will be faced
with the apparent emptiness of the claims that faith makes

> *In certain moods,
> the most dedicated
> believer will be
> faced with the
> apparent emptiness
> of the claims that
> faith makes*

and will have to decide whether or not
to cling to the hope of another kind of
sense, not simply available for inspec-
tion by the casual observer. In certain
moods Lewis believed passionately in
the objective truth of revelation, but he
also knew that at times that truth is
most clearly witnessed to by those who
cling to it without hope of reward or vindication. Once again,
we are in risky territory; but no one could say that we were
being offered a bland or consoling version of faith.

No other stream

Aslan's wildness emerges in this sort of context as the deeply
threatening invitation to a commitment that cannot guarantee anything. This is memorably found in one of Lewis's
most compellingly dreamlike scenes, early in *Silver Chair*
(Ch. 2). Jill, newly arrived in Narnia for the first time, is
alone and desperately thirsty; ahead of her there is a stream
of clear water – and 'just on this side of the stream lay the
Lion'. 'If you're thirsty you may drink,' says the Lion. But Jill

is afraid. 'Will you promise not to – do anything to me, if I do come?' she asks; and the Lion replies, 'I make no promises.'

> Jill was so thirsty now that, without noticing it, she had come a step nearer.
>
> '*Do* you eat girls?' she said.
>
> 'I have swallowed up girls and boys, women and men, kings and emperors, cities and realms,' said the Lion. It didn't say this as if it were boasting, nor as if it were sorry, nor as if it were angry. It just said it.
>
> 'I daren't come and drink,' said Jill.
>
> 'Then you will die of thirst,' said the Lion.
>
> 'Oh dear!' said Jill, coming another step nearer. 'I suppose I must go and look for another stream then.'
>
> 'There is no other stream,' said the Lion.   (pp. 557–8)

Aslan makes no promise; nothing can make him safe, and there is no approaching him without an overwhelming sense of risk. But there is no other stream. A less fearful and guilty person than Jill might – like the talking horse Hwin in *The Horse* (Ch. 14, p. 299) – conclude that 'I'd rather be eaten by you than fed by anyone else.' But one thing Aslan cannot do is pretend he is not what and who he is. Under his scrutiny the likelihood is that we shall all feel as

Aslan makes no promise; nothing can make him safe, and there is no approaching him without an overwhelming sense of risk

unsafe as it is possible to be. In this crucial sense – and as it were in response to the doubts expressed in *Last Battle* – Aslan cannot break his laws. He is not bound by anything except what and who he is, but that is a real and unbreakable bond. He cannot be other than truth. And confronted with truth in this shape, there may be no promises, no rewards and no security, but there is nowhere else to go. Trust in Aslan may even open up the horrific possibilities of corruption and nightmare that *Last Battle* describes, but there is no way for Aslan to come into this world without such risks. There are no other options for truthfulness to enter our consciousness or, more importantly, for sacrificial love to break our chains.

The agonizing uncertainty that all this can generate is brought to the fore in another memorable and controversial passage, towards the end of *Magician's Nephew*. Digory – the future Professor Kirke in whose house the magic wardrobe is located – has been given the task by Aslan of fetching an apple from a distant garden so that its seed may be planted and grow into a tree that will protect Narnia in ages to come. Once in the garden, he is confronted, to his surprise, by the Witch, Jadis (who has already eaten an apple): she tries to persuade him that he must take an apple not for himself but for his seriously ill mother. 'One bite of that apple would heal her' (Ch. 13, p. 93). Or would he prefer – at the cost of his mother's life – to 'run messages for a wild animal in a strange world that is no business of yours?' If Aslan makes Digory refuse the chance of healing his mother, what kind of being is he? Surely 'something worse' even than a wild animal (p. 94).

Digory holds fast to his promise to Aslan (typically, the Witch overplays her hand by suggesting that he could always leave his companion Polly behind when he goes back to his own world so that no one will know of his broken promise – a good instance of what I earlier called the tone-deafness of evil). He returns, hands over the apple, and admits to Aslan that he was tempted not only to take an apple for himself but to take one for his mother. Aslan explains that an apple stolen in such circumstances would have soured the lives of Digory and his mother so much that they 'would have looked back and said it would have been better to die in that illness' (Ch. 13, p. 100).

This episode has drawn a certain amount of criticism.[10] Is Aslan saying that Digory's mother would have been *punished* for his disobedience? Is he being asked to put his loyalty to the Lion above his natural affections? Isn't the whole thing a dangerous bit of moral overloading for a child in any case? There is no doubt that this is – and is obviously meant to be – a difficult bit of the story. But the notion that Digory is in some way manipulated by a threat to his mother, or that he is directly asked to 'sacrifice' her, is to misread what is going on. Digory has already had to set aside a momentary wild idea that he might offer to help Aslan only on condition that his mother is healed (Ch. 12, p. 83). It is the Witch who introduces the idea that Digory should break his promise for his mother's sake; Aslan makes no threat. As he explains, the fruit will work only when plucked and eaten at the right moment or in the right way. Jadis has eaten it in her lust for immortality, and her wish is granted – but it will bring her only misery; she is condemned to eternity in the company of her own boundless selfishness, and it will be torment (p. 100). So whatever would have come from Digory plucking the apple for his mother could not have been good; and Digory recognizes 'that there might be things more terrible even than losing someone you love by death' (ibid.).

Things are as they are. In *The Lion*, Aslan cannot 'work against' the Deep Magic that demands sacrifice as the price of mercy (Ch. 13, p. 176). 'Do you think', he asks Lucy in *Dawn Treader*, 'I wouldn't obey my own rules?' (Ch. 10, p. 498). He cannot make an act of selfishness produce contentment – hence the fate of Queen Jadis. He cannot even make an act of betrayal, however apparently minor, the source of happiness – hence the description of what might have happened to Digory's mother if he had picked an apple for her. It is the other side, the rather terrifying other side, of Aslan's anarchy and subversion. Human rules are neither here nor there, and they are commonly used for unjust purposes; Lewis is enough of a Tory anarchist to be very sceptical of most *schemes* for human happiness. But the real world, which human convention normally obscures for us, is indeed law-governed. Things in the world have a real nature and their effects are according to that nature. *Acts* have a character and their effects are determined by that character. So we must not confuse the anarchic grace that overcomes self-made bonds and human power games with an anarchy that simply denies what is there. Lewis echoes the insight of Bishop Butler, the great eighteenth-century moralist who saw the greatest and most dangerous delusion of human agents as the belief that the consequences of my actions shall be as I please.

> *Human rules are neither here nor there, and they are commonly used for unjust purposes*

What is not easy for us to grasp is that the rule of Aslan is not a matter of arbitrary commands imposed from outside, but of respect for the existence of a world in which things are made (by Aslan) to have real solidity and continuity and our actions have real and creative consequences – even if those creative consequences create what we did not intend or want. The world in which Aslan is ruler is one where healing does not happen through the denial of the truth of things. Yes, it is a 'magical' realm, and Aslan and others have 'magical' powers. But behind all this is what might seem a quite austere picture. Ultimately, the dense and tough structure of reality must be respected – whether it is the structure of the nature that things have or the structure of human acts and choices. What is devilish – and we shall be coming back to this point – is the illusion that we can somehow control this reality by denying it.

There is no other stream. The way to life or reconciliation or forgiveness or renewal is always a path through what is *there*, including, as we shall see in the next chapter, what is there in our own past. And this makes sense only in the context of Aslan's commitment to what has been made: the divine faithfulness is shown in respect for Creation itself in all its diversity, not in a magical capacity to make what is true untrue. Aslan cannot make himself other than he is; he cannot make saltwater fresh, and if we elect to drink saltwater, he cannot make the consequences other than they are. He will do all he can to persuade us not to drink, but that is something else. Understanding this dimension of the religious and moral vision of Narnia is anything but straight-forward in the sort of cultural and intellectual environment we live in (though it was not exactly easy in Lewis's own lifetime). If joy is thought of *first* as the gratification of the will, we are hardly likely to grasp the idea that it is only 'solid' and 'lasting' (in the words of a familiar hymn) if it is the fruit of a participation in what is not the will or the ego – if it is what comes from the contact with something radic-ally other, whether finite or infinite in its otherness. Lewis wants to persuade us that we are to find our fulfilment in receiving rather than in demanding. But there is no honest way of depicting this in fiction except by portraying its risks, the 'wildness' of a world we have not chosen, not to mention a Creator we have not chosen. Perhaps the importance Lewis gives to

> *We are to find our fulfilment in receiving rather than in demanding*

sheer physical enjoyment is a strategic weapon in this context; he is always clear that the plain denial of the flesh (as opposed to all those disciplines that make life in the flesh meaningful) is a betrayal of faith.

But this takes us back to our earlier point about Lewis's narrative tactics, especially in *The Lion*. To begin with we are brought into a world where there is a kind of layer between ourselves and reality – the never-melting snow of Narnia under the Witch's rule. The possibility of joy is bound up with the sense of something between us and the world melting away – and with the joyful subversion that can entail in a world where many or most seem to have an investment in maintaining the layer of unreality. Like his heroes among the great children's authors, Lewis wants to create a certain sense of conspiracy between writer and reader; and this is intensified many times over by being linked to the romance of the return of an exiled king. But reconnection with reality has a price: the liberator is not safe (only 'good'), and his unsafeness is both a carnival of liberation and a relentless austerity, the sheer inescapability of what he is and what he asks. The price of encountering reality, we might say, is precisely the recognition that there isn't an alternative to it. And the challenge is whether we can believe that, often in spite of appearances, it is a well-spring of joy. Hardest of all is when the very vehicles of faith or trust seem to become empty, and worse; and Lewis does not shrink from showing us in painful detail just how this can happen and how it is necessary to hold on to what may *feel* like – at best – a deeply uncertain vision, haunted by all the ingenious ways in which it can be distorted and turned into falsehood.

'No other stream': Aslan cannot make truth untrue, nor can he make human beings instinctively or infallibly truthful. But if we let him he can slowly get us used to truth if we are able to step out beyond our fears – usually, like Jill, not even noticing that this is what we are doing.

4

No story but your own

Aslan loves his world and yet he cannot spare it – in the sense that he cannot make the experience of meeting him easy for persons who habitually settle for much less than the truth in their account of themselves and their world. And one of the simplest and most popular distractions we have developed so as not to have to cope with the truth about ourselves is to spend time and energy looking at others and *their* failings. A recurring theme in Narnia is the warning not to be lured away in this fashion from the actual moment and from our own specific condition. It is part of Aslan's sometimes unwelcome *respect* for the reality he has created that he will not allow us either to comfort or to console ourselves by thinking ourselves into alternative

> *Our choices have been what they have been and have made us what we now are*

histories. Things are as they are; our choices have been what they have been and have made us what we now are; there is nowhere else to begin.

The Horse and His Boy is perhaps the least well known of the books, largely because it introduces characters we do not meet in any other of the stories, though we do meet the four Pevensie children from *The Lion*, grown up and ruling Narnia. The neglect is unjustified; it is a lively and (as we saw in the last chapter) often funny story, despite the discomfort arising from Lewis's stereotypes. Shasta, the young hero, has run away from Calormen accompanied by a very argumentative talking horse and an equally argumentative young Calormene aristocrat, Aravis, who is running away from an unwelcome arranged marriage. Along the road there are various encounters with apparently dangerous lions. When at last Shasta comes face to face with Aslan, he is told that each of these moments has been a meeting with him. In one of these encounters, Aravis has been wounded; Shasta asks, 'Then it was you who wounded Aravis?' and asks what for. 'Child,' Aslan replies, 'I am telling you your own story, not hers. I tell no-one any story but his own' (*The Horse* Ch. 11, p. 281).

Not long afterwards, Aravis too meets Aslan and he explains these wounds: they are the equivalent of the suffering Aravis has caused to her stepmother's slave-girl by her flight from home. Will this slave suffer further because of her, Aravis wants to know. And Aslan replies again, 'I am telling you your story, not hers' (Ch. 14, p. 299). What does Aravis *need* to know? Not information about what is happening in her absence but the nature of her responsibility for someone else's suffering. Aslan will never simply divulge information: at the end of *Dawn Treader*, when Lucy asks whether Eustace will return to Narnia, Aslan's response is,

> We need to know what we have done, in all its dimensions

'Do you really need to know that?' (*Dawn Treader* Ch. 16, p. 541). We need to know what we have done, in all its dimensions. Only Aslan can tell us that; but Aslan will tell us *only* that.

Owning the past

This telling is itself not a matter of information – though, as with Aravis's discovery of the suffering she has inflicted, you could say that we have to assimilate at least some more knowledge in some cases. It is more often and more importantly a question of allowing ourselves to see what we already know, at a level we try to ignore. When Peter, Susan and Lucy speak with Aslan about Edmund in Chapter 12 of *The Lion*, 'something made Peter say' that he is partly responsible for Edmund's desertion: 'I was angry with him and I think that helped him to go wrong.' 'And Aslan said nothing either to excuse Peter or to blame him but merely stood looking at him with his great unchanging eyes. And it seemed to all of them that there was nothing to be said.' There are similar passages in *Magician's Nephew* Chapter 11 (p. 80), where Digory, questioned by Aslan, brings himself to admit that he rang the bell that woke up Queen Jadis from her enchanted sleep, and in *Silver Chair* Chapter 2 (p. 558), where Jill has to confess that Eustace's fall over the cliff is partly the result of her 'showing off'. In both cases, we first hear the kind of self-justification or evasion that any of us would normally offer when a disaster has happened for which we know we share some responsibility: Aslan does not *challenge* this; he simply waits, holding the speaker's gaze, until it is possible, bit by bit, to say more. The admission of responsibility does not bring punishment. It simply opens up the next stage in a conversation with Aslan that will not move forward until we have forced truth out of our mouths – not because we are being ruthlessly interrogated but simply because we *cannot move* until this happens.

How long this takes and what – to use the expression again – it 'feels like' in detail is precisely what Lewis is not going to tell us; it would be the kind of indulgence he has already challenged, wanting to know someone else's story.

Thus in *The Lion* Chapter 13 (p. 174) Edmund's conversation with Aslan is out of earshot: 'There is no need to tell you (and no one ever heard) what Aslan was saying.' Returning to the others, Aslan only says, 'There is no need to talk to him about what is past.' The others are awkward and inarticulate (they are very English children, when all's said and done), but they do not, mercifully, have to discuss or analyse the forgiveness that Edmund has received; they only need (notice how that word recurs) to know that it has happened. Some of this may reflect what was undoubtedly Lewis's own temperamental aversion to anything like self-analysis. Owen Barfield, who knew Lewis as well as any other human being for much of his life, wrote of the mature Lewis[1] that 'self-knowledge, for him, had come to mean recognition of his own weaknesses and shortcomings and nothing more'. 'There was nothing to be said', beyond the fact of culpability and the fact of forgiveness.

The same pattern can be seen, depicted with almost comic brevity, in *Last Battle*, in the meeting between Aslan and the wretched donkey, Puzzle, who has been persuaded by the ape to dress up as Aslan. It is an encounter which occurs, interestingly, almost at the very end of the book, after the long and rapturously described ascent 'further up and further in' towards the ultimate homeland:

And the very first person whom Aslan called to him was Puzzle the Donkey. You never saw a donkey look feebler and sillier that Puzzle did as he walked up to Aslan, and he looked, beside Aslan, as small as a kitten looks beside a St Bernard. The Lion bowed down his head and whispered something to Puzzle at which his long ears went down, but then he said something else at which the ears perked up again. The humans could not hear what he had said either time.

(Ch. 16, p. 766)

Like Edmund, Puzzle has been an agent of real catastrophe and suffering; there is no way in which his complicity can be overlooked, any more than with Edmund. But here, at the narrative climax of a particularly intense series of episodes, this agent of deception and manipulation is welcomed and absolved – once again, out of earshot, because the most important and transforming words Aslan can say are regularly out of earshot. It is a reminder that there is a way to heaven from the gates of hell – surely a deliberate turning upside down of the episode at the end of Bunyan's *Pilgrim's Progress*, where Ignorant is rejected from heaven. Puzzle is indeed 'ignorant', a stupid and gullible creature whose guilt has been incurred by someone else's ambitions; but his responsibility is still utterly real. And yet Aslan deals with this before anything else. We can't be

> *There is a way to heaven from the gates of hell*

sure; but I suspect that Lewis is here reinforcing a point familiar from St Augustine – that most sins are actually *not* dramatic acts of defiance but a half-conscious and certainly half-witted drift towards falsehood or a course reluctantly undertaken out of feebleness and cowardice. Aslan does not despise any of this, nor does he make light of it; he simply deals with it.

The responsible self

If Barfield is right in his analysis of Lewis's own state of mind, and if this is indeed what Lewis is suggesting in these pictures of absolution 'out of earshot', is this an adequate account of sin and forgiveness? In essentials, surely yes: what matters is that the truth is told and the pardon given. Yet we might still ask the question that Barfield hints at: is there some level of maturity missing here? Surely some understanding of where weakness comes from, what triggers or intensifies our sheerly temperamental failings, what kind of self-knowledge would help us grow towards better habits, would not be a waste of time? I doubt whether Lewis would have disagreed exactly; but I think he would also have warned against the risk of substituting self-understanding for actual change. Lewis gives the impression not only in his books but also quite often in his most personal letters that he was not really very interested in himself. Just as he was notoriously uninterested in what he wore and evidently put on the same donnish uniform of shapeless jacket and baggy trousers every morning, so he believed that it was a waste of time to cultivate varied and complex perceptions of oneself as opposed to 'wearing' the same personality without question or hesitation day by day. Religious conversion, he tells us,[2] delivered him from obsessional introspection: 'If Theism had done nothing else for me, I should still be thankful that it cured me of the time-wasting and foolish practice of keeping a diary.' We don't necessarily have to endorse such a judgement on all diary-writing to see the importance of being liberated from certain kinds of obsession about what is 'really' going on in us.

It is in some ways a really admirable and a very un-modern characteristic. But it is quite in tune with another aspect of Lewis that Barfield notes, the ease with which he can slip into 'performance mode'. He was, says Barfield, unable or unwilling to make a sharp distinction between 'I say this' and 'This is the sort of thing a man might say.'[3] It is not part of Lewis's sense of what he has to do to ask, 'Is *this* now the best, the most transparent thing to do or say, the most consistent with what I sense my deepest moral instinct to be?' And in an early letter to Barfield,[4] he discusses the distinction between 'intimacy' and 'familiarity' in a way which allows him to argue that 'intimate' friends do not need to know much about each other in order to be intimate: if a situation arises in which one of the two has to become 'familiar' with the other's history or personal problems, intimacy makes such a sharing possible; but it cannot be the focus of a friendship. In other words, there is never an imperative to expose personal matters to another, and a long-standing and quite deep relationship is quite compatible with a lasting silence on what we usually call 'intimacies'.

This may sound a very odd thing to say about someone who was so manifestly concerned with truthfulness and the unsparing exposure of the self to the light. But it is accurate, I think, to the degree that Lewis did not have very high hopes of finding a level of the personality where these questions could be adequately answered. Assuming a standard *persona* because you can't be bothered with psychological subtleties is not necessarily a form of dishonesty – and this is certainly not what Barfield is suggesting.

> Try as you will, you will not be able to bring out a 'real self' beneath all the outer layers

It is more that, try as you will, you will not be able to bring out a 'real self' beneath all the outer layers. So, rather than spend time and valuable energy on a psychological or spiritual wild-goose chase, simply learn to spot the moments when you are lying or evading what is in front of you, acknowledge your responsibility, seek absolution and move on. It is an ethic and spirituality that looks with great suspicion on any excessive expectations about shared intimacies. Protracted scrutiny of yourself will not yield much more than a set of fresh excuses for more scrutiny; aren't there more important things to get on with?

It is an attitude that explains something of Lewis's carelessness about style and even consistency in the Narnia books and elsewhere in his imaginative writings.[5] And it is what lies near the heart of Aslan's 'no story but your own'. What I may discover about my responsibility is no one's business but mine and God's, and primarily God's. I am called to be truthful about what I *do*; I think Lewis would have said that the supposed call to be truthful about what I *am* was a dangerously indulgent matter, since I could deceive myself almost indefinitely and create all sorts of small and not-so-small dramas around it.

Openness to God

A powerful corrective to some trends, certainly; not a point of view to take uncritically, as there has to be some morally

significant connection between what I do and what I am –
and Lewis in some moods would clearly recognize this. But
to be aware of this side of him as a moralist is important
in reading Narnia with full attention and sympathy. And
it throws some light on another memorable episode in the
books, the account of Eustace's transformation in *Dawn
Treader*. The thoroughly obnoxious Eustace, censorious, vain
and cowardly, finds himself turned into a dragon after an
unfortunate encounter with some enchanted gold (Ch. 6).
He is subsequently rescued by Aslan, and his description
of this process as mediated through a sort of dream is one
of Lewis's most metaphorically rich ventures. Although
Eustace tries to shut his eyes against Aslan's gaze, he cannot
resist his call to follow (p. 474). He is taken to a garden
where there is a well in which he is told to bathe; but first
he must 'undress'. He scratches off his scales, so he thinks,
peeling off his outer skin – and then sees his reflection and
realizes that he is still wearing the dragon's hide. He peels
off another layer and another, but to no avail. 'Then the Lion
said . . . "You will have to let me undress you"' (p. 474).

The Lion's claws cut so deeply that the hurt is 'worse than
anything I've ever felt'. The dragon's skin is at last peeled off
completely, and the Lion tosses Eustace into the well and
reclothes him. He is human again, conscious of the rawness

of his skin yet delighted to see his own body once more, despite its relative weakness and unimpressiveness (p. 475).

The baptismal imagery is obvious and doesn't need labouring; but what is significant is that the rediscovery of human identity is not something that we can do in our own strength; we shall always be tempted to stop before we get to the deepest level and so always liable to imagine we have 'arrived' when we haven't. Only Aslan's claws can strip away the entire clothing of falsehood with which we have surrounded ourselves. And I think that this casts light on Lewis's scepticism about self-analysis: it will always be incomplete and it will always be shadowed by our longing to arrive at a satisfying stopping-place.

So what is required is not that we bravely go on undertaking more and more complex explorations into the ego, only that we declare to God our willingness to be stripped. Once again, this has echoes – intentional or not – of St John of the Cross and the acceptance of the night of the spirit and its stripping of the self down to its naked truth. And it more deliberately echoes some of the themes elaborated in *The Great Divorce*, where just the same profoundly painful tearing away of the masks and dramas of the self is imagined for souls in Purgatory.[6] 'However many skins do I have to take off?' asks Eustace. We cannot answer for ourselves. We can only signal that we want help to be stripped in this way. And, as we have seen so often in earlier discussion, Aslan cannot protect us from the pain this entails. There are two non-negotiable things in contact here – the unalterable character of Aslan himself on the one hand, and the irreversible actuality of what we have done or what we have made of ourselves on the other. The former cannot change; only the latter can. And it can change only by being laid open in one way or another to the energy and action of the former.

We may not want to change; in which case, we are indeed frozen, perpetually frustrated. We are not *punished* for our recalcitrance, as if by an outside agency imposing a penalty – only left with ourselves in a 'length of misery' (*Magician's Nephew* Ch. 14, p. 100). Going back for a moment to the fate of Susan as touched on in *Last Battle*, we'd have to say that she is in no sense punished for particular things she has done or may do: but she is in the process of becoming a certain kind of person, a certain kind of 'grown-up'. And for such people the journey back to nakedness and forgiveness is likely to be hard. There will be quite a lot of skins for Aslan to remove. But, as *The Great Divorce* repeatedly insists, the only *decision* to be a stranger to heaven is ours.

> We may not want to change; in which case, we are indeed frozen, perpetually frustrated

Once such a decision is made and once it becomes a habit of mind, the persistent work of God to break through is bound to be experienced as an assault on the citadel of the soul rather than a campaign to liberate that soul from its self-imposed captivity (we shall see later in this chapter how this particular theme is captured in the Narnia stories). God cannot but start from the situation as it is, as we have seen, with acts performed, habits shaped, actual events having happened (Aslan does not tell us what would have happened; the nearest we come to this – and the circumstances are unusual – is Aslan telling Digory of what might have happened to his mother and himself had he taken the apple).

What or who are we 'under the skin'? Lewis is reluctant to give any room to the idea that we could ever answer such a question. In a very specific sense, he is as hostile to the notion of a 'real self' underlying the flux of experience as any deconstructionist critic or psychoanalyst. But this is not because he wants to dissolve the substance of the soul into sensations and linguistic detached performances. On the contrary; the soul or self is uncomfortably real. We discover just how uncomfortable when we are faced with what we have done in the presence of complete Truthfulness. But it is only in relation to that Truthfulness that we can be said to *have* a real self – not a hidden level of consciousness that, once we find it, will show us what we 'really' ought to do, but a hidden story, the narrative of our lives as seen by the eye of God. In the nature of the case, we have no access to this except *in* the eye of God.

For Lewis, this meant that what commonly passed for self-awareness or self-examination was something of a delusion. All we can hope for is a habit of prosaic honesty, ready to learn over and over again where we have been deceived by ourselves or others. 'As long as we have the itch of self-regard,' he wrote in a letter of 1954, 'we shall want the pleasure of self-approval; but the happiest moments are those when we forget our precious selves and have neither but have everything else (God, our fellow humans, animals, the garden and the sky) instead.'[7] And developing the habit of undeceiving ourselves so that we are free from self-regard and self-approval is inseparable from the habit of openness to God, openness without 'agenda', a plain willingness to receive what is given, co-existing with a peaceable agnosticism about who I really am – a question whose resolution is indisputably and solely in the hands of God.

So we are not supposed, Lewis believes, to focus our attention too closely on the unanswerable question of our 'real' nature: it will come to light – as much as we need to know of it – in the process of engaging with Aslan and his world.

What matters most is being made able to see the bare facts of what you have done and the effects of it – which may involve, as with Aravis, learning by unpleasant experience about the suffering casually caused to others. This is (perhaps surprisingly) the closest we come in Narnia to Aslan inflicting a straightforward *punishment*, as opposed to leaving the wicked with the consequences for themselves of their choices. But it is simply an aspect of knowing what your acts really entail. When Aravis first tells Shasta the story of her escape from home, she 'coolly' assumes that the servant girl whom she has drugged will be beaten: and 'she was doubtless a tool and spy of my stepmother's. I am very glad they should beat her.' Shasta protests at this unfairness, and Aravis replies, 'I did not do any of these things for the sake of pleasing *you*' (Ch. 3, p. 224). Aravis at this point cannot imagine a scale for measuring actions that is not concentrated entirely on her own desires. But she is not an actively bad person: she is evidently capable of receiving and understanding the wounds given her by Aslan, growing into and through the new awareness of what she has done, and she makes a good end as Queen of Archenland.

We do need to know what our actions entail as a bare matter of fact; we do not need to know more. As we have already seen, human beings will regularly deceive themselves not only about what they have actually done but about the effects of it. In *The Lion* Peter has to face the fact in Aslan's presence that his own ill-temper played its part in Edmund's betrayal; he volunteers this, we must suppose, as a direct result of meeting Aslan and no more; Aravis needs a bit more encouragement to make the leap into another's place and another's pain. Self-deceit may be the broadly comic thing

> *Human beings will regularly deceive themselves not only about what they have actually done but about the effects of it*

we see in Eustace's diary in *Dawn Treader* (Ch. 2, pp. 437–8), where he writes up the events of the voyage from the point of view of a sheltered, pampered and smug twentieth-century boy; the nicest touch is when he quotes his father saying 'one of the most cowardly things ordinary people do is to shut their eyes to Facts'. His own pitiful attempts to force his Narnian experience into the categories of a progressive contemporary mindset, acquired from his equally smug and sheltered parents (notice the disparaging '*ordinary* people' in Eustace's recollection of his father's wisdom), are narrated by Lewis with some relish. But although this self-deception is corrosive for poor Eustace himself, it is not immediately disastrous for others (however annoying).

Corporate delusions

The destructive thing in all this is the underlying philosophy which has made Eustace what he is. And here Lewis indulges himself mightily in heavy-handed satire at the expense of 'progressive' education. When we meet the chastened Eustace again at the beginning of *Silver Chair*, he has returned to his enlightened school; and Lewis paints a savagely hostile picture of a manipulative, undisciplined environment where bullying goes unchecked and the most physically and psychologically powerful children exercise a reign of terror. Any reader of school stories from *Tom Brown's Schooldays* onwards – let alone memoirs of school life in the early twentieth century, notably including Lewis's own – might want to protest that such an atmosphere seems to be at least as familiar in more traditionally minded establishments. But Lewis is taking the opportunity of striking a blow against that over-optimistic humanism which he saw as the greatest *corporate* self-deceit of the age. Eustace's school is built on dishonesty, the refusal to see that simply giving licence to the young can mean leaving the weakest unprotected (*Lord of the Flies* casts its shadow before it, not to mention a more recent foray into this distressing field, by A. S. Byatt in *Babel Tower*). But that dishonesty rests on the deeper dishonesty of imagining that human instinct left to itself will work for the common good, and that *planned* solutions to human misery (in particular those that rest on this assumption about instincts) are the ideal.

You can appreciate the direction of the satire without endorsing the embarrassingly heavy-handed tactics at the beginning and the end of *Silver Chair*. Lewis is writing out of deeply rooted prejudices that have at least as much to do with his own horrible experiences at preparatory school as with the world of progressive education, of which he can have known little if anything at first hand. And Eustace's parents, with their odd habits (they are *vegetarians*; surely capable of any iniquity), are, just like the children at some points, more obviously inhabitants of an Edwardian world than of postwar England. The ghosts of Bernard Shaw and H. G. Wells are much in evidence here, and the scores Lewis is settling are old ones. Wells, of course, whom Lewis greatly admired as a storyteller and loathed as a philosopher, is mocked with near-libellous ferocity in *That Hideous Strength*, where he appears as the self-educated, self-satisfied Jules, wheeled out by the diabolical plotters of Belbury to adorn a celebratory dinner with his platitudes.

But *That Hideous Strength*, for all the ambivalence it produces even among its admirers, is directed at a better-identified target, the fantasies of a wholly managed society and a technological overriding of nature itself. As Lewis himself perceptively recognized (and noted in the book itself), this is something beyond the ordinary categories of right and left in politics; which is what makes the novel far more than a conservative tract in any ordinary sense. In contrast, the facile mockery of *Dawn Treader* and *Silver Chair* sounds more like uninformed reactionary grumbling; sadly, the broadness of the satire cloaks the extremely significant insights about bullying and about how ideology can blind you to the complexities of children's relations with each other.

But there is one aspect of *That Hideous Strength* which finds a clear and striking echo in Narnia. At one point in the novel, one of the directors of the great programme of Promethean technology at Belbury takes his companion (young Mark, whom we have already met) to the window and points to the moon: there is a world stripped of organic life, rational and *clean*. It is in fact the result of a deliberate campaign of 'purification' by the moon's hidden inhabitants who have 'broken free (almost) from the organic'; and the same effects can be brought about here on earth.[8] The villains of Belbury are the enemies of Creation itself, eager to crush the unpredictability and irrational profusion or organic life whether as expressed in the irrational traditions and allegiances of historical societies or in the natural world. It is no surprise that they are enthusiastic supporters of vivisection (which gives extra colour to Lewis's nightmare vision of 'God the vivisector' in *A Grief Observed*); and the appalling slaughter at the climax of the book is enacted by the abused animals taking their revenge.

The 'iron age' depicted at the beginning of *Last Battle*, as the ape begins to take power in Narnia, is marked by a number of atrocities, including the enslavement of the talking beasts. But the most vivid image is in Chapter 2 with the felling of the trees: the ape is selling timber to the Calormenes, and King Tirian is shocked to see 'a hideous lane like a raw gash in the land, full of muddy ruts where felled trees had been dragged down to the river' (p. 679). This is achieved by forced labour, of course; but still more significantly Tirian is appealed to by the Dryads, the tree-spirits, for protection. They are his *people* (p. 677). The covenant that binds the king to the land is one that involves all sentient beings – with the implication that the Dryads also speak for all the trees in some way, as the talking beasts represent the interests of all the animal world. The coming of the Antichrist in the shape of Shift and Puzzle is signalled by a regime that has no concept of any such covenant. This is in essence the world of Belbury again.

As we saw in Chapter 1, putting humanity in its place is an important aspect of the Narnia stories – both in the obvious negative sense of puncturing human self-confidence and illusory optimism and in the positive sense of reaffirming the unique role of humanity in the history not only of our universe but also of other worlds. Knowing the truth about ourselves, as individuals and as a human race, involves being able to see where we actually are in relation to Creator and Creation. Lewis was an expert in literature that took that kind of knowledge and ability for granted. He also believed with the deepest conviction that modern readers were largely quite incapable of understanding what was at issue here, and it is hard to disagree. His often startling ways of locating humanity in the Narnian cosmos need to be read in the light of this conviction.

Knowing the truth about ourselves involves being able to see where we actually are in relation to Creator and Creation

5

The silent gaze of truth

Being told your story by Aslan doesn't compel your assent. The pain of being confronted with what you have done in all its detail is acute, as we have seen, and it should not surprise us if some will not accept it. In such a case, there is ultimately no solution that Aslan or anyone else can deliver. This is the most austere

> *Being told your story by Aslan doesn't compel your assent*

element in the imaginative world that Lewis creates, and – to underline the point again – it is not about punishment imposed from outside but about what we have made ourselves to be. Lewis is deliberately ambiguous about whether someone who has made himself or herself invulnerable to the appeal of truth can actually become another person, given immeasurable time. *The Great Divorce* allows such a possibility – but it also shows people on the edge of change still drawing back, because they cannot face letting go of some aspect of their self-image.[1] The essential point is the one made by Aslan to Digory about Jadis, a point we have already touched on:

She has won her heart's desire; she has unwearying strength and endless days like a goddess. But length of days with an evil heart is only length of misery and already she begins to know it. All get what they want; they do not always like it.

(*Magician's Nephew* Ch. 15, p. 100)

This is of course a fairly extreme case, a set of choices made out of raging ambition and egotism (most powerfully illustrated in Chapter 5 of *Magician's Nephew*, with Jadis's account of how she destroyed her own world at the end of a colossal and bloody war to prevent her sister's victory; the nearest Lewis gets to a moral comment on the 'Mutually Assured Destruction' of the nuclear arms race?). But one of the challenging things about Narnia – as about *The Great Divorce* – is its insistence that the refusal of the truth may happen not in this high diabolical style but in the accumulation of routine suspicion and selfishness. This is most plainly set out in the history of the dwarfs in *Last Battle*. We have already seen how they jeer at the claims made by Tirian and the children about Aslan, how they mock them for repeating that 'he's not a tame lion'. We also see them firing their arrows indiscriminately at both sides in the battle in Chapter 11: 'We don't want you to win any more than the other gang. The Dwarfs are for the Dwarfs' (p. 733).

In Chapter 13, they find themselves in the stable where the false Aslan has been lodged, now transformed into a doorway to the new world. But they are unable to see that there is light all around them; offered flowers to smell, they insist that it is stable-litter. When Aslan himself produces a feast of good things, 'They began eating and drinking greedily enough, but it was clear that they couldn't taste it properly.' And they promptly start quarrelling; 'every Dwarf began suspecting that every other Dwarf had found something nicer than he had.' When they have settled down, they console themselves with the knowledge that at least they haven't been deceived; 'We haven't let anyone take us in. The Dwarfs are for the Dwarfs.' Aslan comments that 'They have chosen cunning instead of belief. Their prison is only in their own minds, yet they are in that prison; and so afraid of being taken in that they cannot be taken out' (p. 748). And this just recapitulates rather more sombrely the fate of the incompetent magician Uncle Andrew in *Magician's Nephew*: the foolish old man is incapable of understanding what is going on around him as Narnia is called into life, and can only think of what personal advantage it might bring him. Aslan cannot explain,

and I cannot comfort him either; he has made himself unable to hear my voice. If I spoke to him, he would hear only growlings and roarings. Oh, Adam's sons, how cleverly you defend yourselves against all that might do you good!
(*Magician's Nephew* Ch. 14, p. 98)

The temptations of unreality

'He has made himself unable to hear.' It is, in these episodes at the beginning and end of Narnian history, both a comic and a tragic turn of events. The determination to protect the self at all costs leads to a denial of reality, and that denial is basically what hell means, however you dress it up. Towards

> *The determination to protect the self at all costs leads to a denial of reality*

the end of *That Hideous Strength*,[2] we see one of the villains on the point of death struggling to maintain his hold not on reality but on the false conviction he has made himself live with – the illusion that the body and the consciousness are themselves illusions. 'With one supreme effort he flung himself back into this illusion. In that attitude eternity overtook him.' As Aslan implies, both energy and ingenuity are needed to deny what is in front of your nose, and human beings are astonishingly liberal with this energy and ingenuity – until they are unable to do otherwise, or as near unable as we can imagine. Hell may be the torturing self-consciousness of Jadis. It may equally well be a habit of wilful blindness that we more and more refuse to notice – a low-key, half-comic, *perhaps* not eternal hell, but none the less terrible for that, because it is a place of shadows and frustration. Poor Uncle

Andrew at the end of *Magician's Nephew* is 'a nicer and less selfish old man than he had ever been before' (Ch. 15, p. 106), but he still indulges himself with memories of the mysterious foreign royalty (Queen Jadis) he once entertained in London. 'A devilish temper she had . . . But she was a dem fine woman, sir, a dem fine woman.' We can charitably assume that he is possibly on the way to something akin to repentance, even that his self-delusion is not that serious. Yet everything in Narnia tells us that there is, in the long run, no such thing as a harmless delusion. Sooner or later, Uncle Andrew, like the dwarfs, will have to face the possibility of letting go of the stories he tells himself about himself.

> *Everything in Narnia tells us that there is, in the long run, no such thing as a harmless delusion*

Throughout the stories, Lucy is pretty consistently portrayed as a touchstone of courage and clarity. It is all the more striking, then, that she is shown in *Dawn Treader* briefly but intensely facing the temptations of unreality. In Chapter 10, Lucy is leafing through a book of spells, and comes across one that promises to make her 'beautiful beyond the lot of mortals'; she scrutinizes the page, imagining more and more dramatic adventures caused by her beauty (and also imagining Susan 'plainer and with a nasty expression', clearly jealous but now insignificant). But at the last moment the image of Aslan growling at her seems to emerge from the page and she hastily turns onwards (p. 496). Interestingly, the 2009 film intensified this episode in a very effective way: Lucy sees herself endowed with Susan's beauty and is entranced by the thought until she realizes that she has *become* Susan in her fantasy – and Lucy no longer exists. This is the point where she takes fright: her dream has swallowed up her own reality.

She does give way to another temptation, however, which is a spell that will 'let you know what your friends thought about you'. Lucy – predictably – hears a friend apparently patronizing her and promising her affection and attention to another girl, and she is hurt and furious. But when she moves on and utters a spell 'to make hidden things visible', Aslan appears, and she has to confront her foolishness. As Aslan explains, her friend's words were the result of fear and weakness, and did not express what she truly felt. But Lucy cannot forget what she has heard: the friendship is damaged, and there is no way back. She has made the mistake (in Lewis's moral or psychological world) of looking for the wrong kind of intimacy, as Lewis explains in his letter to Barfield on the familiar and the intimate. She has looked for what the other 'really' thinks or feels. But being a spectator of what others say when you are absent in fact doesn't tell you anything of this; it only introduces new complications. As the philosopher Stanley Cavell memorably writes about Shakespeare's *Othello*,[3] Othello's problem is not that he needs and lacks *information* about his wife's true feelings. He is hungry for information of a kind that can never answer his fundamental question – to which the only answers are to be found in the actual *exercise* of love (or in Lucy's case, friendship).

In other words, Lucy has turned away from one temptation to unreality only to fall into another and still more seductive one; she recognizes just in time the spiritually suicidal nature of wanting to replace one's own given reality with another identity, but still seeks to replace the given challenges and uncertainties of human intimacy – including the constantly threatening doubt as to whether I *really* know or am known by the other – with some kind of guarantee, some magical access to the truth. But this is not available, and to seek it is to jeopardize (as in *Othello*) what a relationship actually is between two finite and physical selves. It is as though we have here a glimpse of another kind of 'hell': not straightforwardly the refusal of reality but the refusal to let ordinary human exchange *count* as reality. If we cannot arrive at a completely transparent knowledge of the other – person or thing or, for that matter, God – we shall find that nothing can ever come up to the standards we set for reality. We shall have excluded ourselves from truth because we want an unattainable certainty. We shall be tormented by a hunger for what can never be.

What Narnia has to say about self-knowledge and human maturity is in fact among the most difficult of its messages; put in the abstract terms I have been using here, it would seem pretty well impossible to communicate in a narrative for children. Yet Lewis manages to convey a great deal of complex psychological insight through simple catchphrases and through the poignant and vivid accounts of what meeting Aslan is like – most powerfully, what meeting Aslan is like if you have something to hide. Left to yourself, Lewis says, you will always find good reasons for justifying what you have done. And if what you have done involves damage to another, your justification will bring with it at least some measure of denial of the other's experience, the other's reality. And if you try to assure yourself of your worth or virtue by seeking to 'overhear' what others think of you, you will be at best frustrated and at worst hurt and diminished.

Neither self-analysis nor the hope of seeing your face perfectly and justly reflected in the eyes of a human other will deliver you from the ever-present attraction of fiction over reality. And this leads by implication into what is almost a

kind of moral argument for the existence of God. There is only one means
of deliverance and it is confrontation
with the truth in the form of a living
person who has no distorting lens
of self-interest in their vision of you.
To meet Aslan is to meet someone

> *To meet Aslan is to
> meet someone who
> is free to see you
> as you are and to
> reflect that seeing
> back to you*

who, because he has freely created you and wants for you
nothing but your good, your flourishing, is free to see you
as you are and to reflect that seeing back to you. In his eyes
you can indeed see yourself reflected perfectly and justly.

Surprised by joy

We need for our deliverance a perspective which transcends
the competition of interest and advantages that is the world
of human persons. And while such need is not in itself a
compelling rational argument for the existence of something
that satisfies it, Lewis at least wants us to consider the oddity
of a world in which such a need exists and is doomed to
eternal frustration. It is all of a piece with his repeated
appeal – especially in his autobiography – to the experience
of *joy*. There are moments in our experience when we
know that we are overtaken by a fulfilment of desire so

overwhelmingly more than we could have expected that we can only think of it in terms of contact with a life or an agency immeasurably in *excess* of what we can otherwise imagine. Even the most 'routine' experience of happiness, as Lewis observes in the letter of 1954 quoted earlier in this chapter, involves a degree of self-forgetting; joy is what happens when we are not analysing ourselves. So the strict warnings about the stories we tell ourselves, warnings that may sound to a compulsively self-absorbed age like prescriptions for insensitivity or immaturity, are all to do with giving ourselves the space and the liberty to be 'surprised by joy'. If joy is real and irresistible, if it answers the most serious hunger we have, our need for truth is in fact answered. What we finally see reflected in the face of truth is *both* the depth of our hunger for joy and the tangle of ingenious strategies for avoiding what we most want, strategies that we devise because we fear the dissolving of our self-possession that joy brings with it. The startling, even shocking, response of the horse Hwin to Aslan – 'I'd sooner be eaten by you than fed by anyone else' – is a particularly dramatic way of expressing the acceptance of this dissolution.

Faced with this, some may reach into the cliché-basket for accusations of masochism. But this sits very badly with the obvious fact that pain in Narnia *is* pain, and is unwelcome and avoided whenever it can be. It is just its unwelcome character that drives us to lie and evade when the truth seems to threaten us. To go back again to the letter of 1954: 'If there is an itch one does want to scratch; but it is much nicer to have *neither* the itch nor the scratch.'[4] Given our restless insecurity, our immediate desire to be affirmed without question, we devise ways of assuring ourselves. It may be painful to let go of all this, but what is ultimately promised is precisely an experience that is beyond the itch and the scratch: joy. What is significant is not the pain itself but something more serious – expressed perhaps in a moment like the one we have already touched on when Peter accepts his responsibility for Edmund's betrayal. 'Aslan said nothing either to excuse Peter or to blame him . . . And it seemed to all of them that there was nothing to be said.'

Judgement is something that happens in silence; silence is what judgement creates. And what is silenced is the passion to make my story utterly and finally my own, to tell it to myself, uninterrupted. Aslan's silence interrupts; and only in that moment can I hear or see my story as it is and might be. When in Chapter 14 of *Last Battle*

> *Judgement is something that happens in silence; silence is what judgement creates*

all the creatures of Narnia swarm through the stable door into Aslan's presence, 'They all looked straight in his face, I don't think they had any choice about that' (p. 751). When they see him, some hate what they see and disappear into his long shadow: 'I don't know what became of them,' says Lewis simply. Others look and are terrified, but still love what they see – even one of the dwarfs who before has been hostile. All are, so to speak, *unmasked* in this presence; what determines their immediate fate is whether they can bear the fear and the pain of Aslan's silent gaze. In Chapter 15, the young Calormene soldier who has bravely walked into the stable because he believes that he will meet there the god whom he loves – although it is the false god of Calormen – describes his meeting with Aslan, who explains that all honest service done to the false god is counted as service to him (just as all dishonest or cruel acts done in Aslan's name are counted as service to the diabolical Tash). Aslan says to the soldier that 'unless thy desire had been for me thou wouldst not have sought so long and so truly' – almost a direct quotation from St Augustine. What ultimately matters is desire for truth, whatever the cost; but that desire is only met in the face of the true God and in letting him tell you your story. It is no

What ultimately matters is desire for truth, whatever the cost

accident that the Calormene soldier is called Emeth – the Hebrew word for 'truth'.

This unmasking is what we must hope for, and that is what we must not try and anticipate by what we – noisily and compulsively – say to ourselves. How far Lewis's temperamental reserve, the sense that he is giving a 'performance' that Barfield hints at, enters in here is very hard to assess. But even allowing for the fact that Lewis was instinctively wary of anything that could look like emotional self-indulgence, even if his insights are marked by a stoicism that was both typical of him and typical of a generation, there is a perfectly serious moral and spiritual challenge here to any philosophy or ethic that misunderstands the purpose of searching for self-knowledge. What finally separates the Narnian vision from any kind of stoicism is the bare fact of Lewis's focus on joy as the rationale of all properly human endeavour and experience: self-knowledge means the knowledge of how we intrude the self we *imagine* between our actual prosaic developing reality and the joy that is promised us.

6

Bigger inside than outside

*It's – it's a magic wardrobe. There's a wood inside it,
and it's snowing, and there's a Faun and a Witch
and it's called Narnia; come and see.*

(*The Lion* Ch. 3, p. 120)

Lucy's summary of the mystery introduces us to the image
that will recur at the end of the stories: we go through a
door into a reality that is bigger than the one we have left
behind; the world opens out, it shows itself to be 'bigger on
the inside than the outside'. As the final catastrophe over-
whelms Narnia, the stable where Shift the ape has hidden
the false Aslan – Puzzle the donkey, wearing his tattered
lion skin – becomes unexpectedly just such a door into the
depths. At first it appears that it is a doorway into torment
and death: the demonic god of Calormen lives there, and
will devour everything that steps through the door. But
suddenly, when King Tirian has entered, it is transformed:
the heroes of the other stories (minus Susan, as we have seen)
advance to meet him, and Tirian realizes that he is indeed

in a different realm. 'The Stable seen from within and the Stable seen from without are two different places,' he says; and Lucy adds that 'In our world too, a Stable once had something inside it that was bigger than our whole world' (*Last Battle* Ch. 13, p. 744) – an unusually (though not quite uniquely) direct reference to the Christian story.

More is to come, though. This new world is in fact Narnia – only its mountains are higher, its colours more intense: 'they're more . . . more . . . oh, I don't know,' says Lucy; and Digory 'softly' supplies, 'More like the real thing' (Ch. 15, p. 759). By this time, the familiar Narnia has been destroyed in the apocalyptic desolation of Chapter 14, where, in an extraordinary image, the giant Father Time 'took the sun and squeezed it in his hand as you would squeeze an orange' (p. 753). But here is Narnia again, larger than life and twice as natural. Digory – Professor Kirke as an adult, remember – offers his explanation. Narnia as we have known it is a copy of the 'real' Narnia, and all that 'mattered' in the Narnia we have known is here in its original integrity and beauty. 'It's all in Plato, all in Plato: bless me, what *do* they teach them at these schools?' (p. 759).

Everything we know is a copy of 'something in Aslan's real world', England no less than Narnia. So the further we go into Aslan's world, the more vivid becomes our apprehension of what has mattered in our own world. It is indeed 'Platonism' in the sense that our familiar world is understood as a reflection of something more lasting and solid. But Lewis takes the *solidity* of the Platonic world in an entirely fresh way. It is not that the solid beauties and joys of the present

> *The further we go into Aslan's world, the more vivid becomes our apprehension of what has mattered in our own world*

are to be sacrificed in the name of 'higher' realities that are more spiritual – not unless we drastically revise what we normally mean by 'spiritual'. Aslan's world is, you could say, more *material* than ours: its sensory delights are more intense.

A deeper country

The journey to this true homeland (and the echoes of St Augustine are as strong as those of Plato) is not a journey away from the world we know but one into its heart. 'The new one was a deeper country' (Ch. 15, p. 760). And as the friends travel at Aslan's prompting towards the earthly paradise visited by Digory in *Magician's Nephew*, the garden beyond the Western Wild where the healing tree grows, they are joined by all who have shared their adventures; all the memories they have had are reclaimed. Inside the paradisal garden, the same theme is repeated: this too is 'bigger inside than it was outside' (Ch. 16, p. 765), containing a Narnia still more real and beautiful than even the transfigured Narnia they entered through the stable door: 'like an onion: except that as you go in and in, each circle is larger than the last' (ibid.). And the final dimension of this vision is revealed as they see that beyond the frontiers of this heavenly Narnia is a heavenly England, with all that they think they have lost (including the Pevensie parents) restored. And Mr Tumnus from *The Lion* explains that all these *real* countries or worlds 'are only spurs jutting out from the great mountains of Aslan' (p. 766). To go on 'upwards and inwards' through any of these worlds is finally to arrive in Aslan's homeland.

The richness of these concluding pages of *Last Battle* is a heady and challenging diet for a reader of any age. But to grasp what it is presenting is to grasp what is one of the most significant elements not only in the Narnia stories but in the whole of Lewis's work. Just as when we meet Aslan we are put in touch with what is solid in ourselves (and obliged to let go of what is false), just as we are stripped of our private versions of reality in order to be fed with the joy of truth itself, so with our experience of the entire world we inhabit. Once we have left behind our self-centred perspective, what is opened out to us is a fuller not a smaller field of enjoyment; the world itself becomes more 'intense' in its impact, and we sense (literally *sense*) dimensions to the world that we should otherwise never have encountered.

> *Once we have left behind our self-centred perspective, what is opened out to us is a fuller not a smaller field of enjoyment*

It is all of a piece with Lewis's insistence that the traditional Christian world view does not entail some kind of emptying-out of familiar material reality in favour of a ghostly substitute: it is this world which is so often a ghostly substitute for the real thing because of our own fear of what is real. Behind his images in *Last Battle* are the early Christian and mediaeval notions of the 'spiritual senses', the recreation in the spiritual realm of the variegated experiences that come to us through the physical senses – but given an original and very robust imaginative flavour. Although I doubt whether Lewis had ever encountered the thought of the seventh-century theologian, Maximus the Confessor,[1] Maximus' conception of each created thing resting upon a distinct 'word' or possible ideal form contained in the single action of God the Word offers a notable parallel to the picture of all the 'ideal' countries/worlds joined like ridges or spurs to the single mountain range that is Aslan's country. And it should also be remembered that Lewis had, by the time he wrote the Narnia books, digested many of the theological ideas of his close friend Charles Williams,[2] who had underlined so strongly the importance of the 'way of Affirmation of Images' – the belief that our *positive* images of God represent more than we can otherwise speak of, so that the divine reality must not be thought of only in terms of what it is not, of what our language cannot ever capture, but imagined also as that which contains, in infinite 'excess', all that we say about what is good or beautiful in the immediate objects we experience.

Lewis had experimented with a number of ways to express this in earlier works. *The Great Divorce* shows us the spirits of the lost and the unreal walking on grass that 'did not bend under their feet', trying to pick up leaves that feel 'heavier than a sack of coal' to them, because these things are so solid in comparison with their flimsiness; and at the end, the narrator feels light falling on him 'like solid blocks, intolerable of edge and weight'.[3] And in *That Hideous Strength* one of the characters sketches a similar idea to *Last Battle*'s picture of the 'true' countries that connect to Aslan's country: he speaks of an inner, truer reality in the various countries of the world, all nations being 'haunted' by an elusive ideal of spiritual and moral identity which can be corrupted or transfigured, depending on the actual choices of its citizens at any one time. 'The whole work of healing Tellus [the earth] depends on nursing that little spark, on incarnating that ghost, which is still alive in every real people, and different in each.'[4] *The Great Divorce* also plays with the notion of relative size – we discover at the end that the whole of 'hell' is contained in a microscopic crevice, so that the journey to heaven is one of scale, not distance. As in *Last Battle*, the point is that the world when seen in relation to Aslan is larger than it would otherwise be or appear, and to refuse this vision is to condemn yourself to an unending shrinkage. The point is caught memorably and simply in *Prince Caspian* Chapter 10, when Lucy meets Aslan again for the first time since the events of *The Lion*.

> 'Aslan,' said Lucy, 'you're bigger.'
> 'That is because you are older, little one,' answered he.
> 'Not because you are?'
> 'I am not. But every year you grow, you will find me bigger.' (p. 380)

A bigger faith

The more we develop, the more there is to see and know of Aslan. Lewis is determined to turn on its head the common

> *The more we develop, the more there is to see and know of Aslan*

assumption that faith is one of those things that the intelligent human will simply grow out of: on the contrary, we shall be constantly growing into it, without end. Part of this growing also means that the habits of faith that served us well at earlier stages may not survive untouched. As the conversation between Lucy and Aslan continues, Lucy admits ruefully that she had hoped Aslan would 'come roaring in and frighten all the enemies away', as he had done before (in *The Lion*); but he warns her that 'things never happen the same way twice' (p. 381). Now she has to take the responsibility of letting the others know what Aslan wants, and, if necessary, to follow alone if they will not listen. When she agrees and feels 'lion-strength' flowing in, Aslan says, significantly, 'Now you are a lioness.' Instead of Aslan coming in to solve everything in dramatic and visible ways, Lucy must take the part of Aslan: her faith must cope with a new situation in which the old and straightforward resolutions fade away and new risks appear. Yet it is equally plain that this is made possible by a vivid sense that Aslan's sheer presence is what it always was.

'Every year you grow, you will find me bigger'; but this involves finding Aslan also stranger or more demanding as time passes. Lewis, here as elsewhere, hints strongly at the necessary movement of faith beyond the images we have found comforting in the past. To cling to those pictures is to refuse growth – and so to refuse the fulfilment that exceeds what can now be imagined. All of this is captured, with tantalizing brevity, in Chapter 10 of *Dawn Treader*, once again in Lucy's visit to the magician's house. She comes across a spell 'for the refreshment of the spirit', and reads with total absorption; but when she wants to turn the pages back, she cannot, and her memory of it begins to fade. 'Let's see . . . it was about . . . about . . . oh dear, it's all fading away again . . . How can I have forgotten? It was about a cup and a sword and a tree and a green hill, I know that much. But I can't remember' (p. 497). When Aslan appears, Lucy rather timidly asks, 'Shall I ever be able to read that story again: the one I couldn't remember? Will you tell it to me, Aslan? Oh do, do, do.' And Aslan replies that he 'will tell it you for years and years' (p. 498).

Reading the story has felt like living in it 'as if it were real, and all the pictures were real too'; and for ever after, the measure of a good story for Lucy is that it reminds her of this forgotten tale (p. 497). It is, clearly, the story of how grace interweaves with our own lives – literally, how the spirit is refreshed. The cup, the sword, the tree and the hill are all images and narratives from the gospel, but reduced to these telegraphic symbols because as such they can be echoed and rediscovered again and again in new situations, new stories, as the spirit is renewed and anchored again and again in the one story of God's dealings with the world. There is no turning back, no access to what might have been; but the story will go on being told if we are able to listen to Aslan. And at the very end of the Narnia saga, on the last page of *Last Battle*, this image returns. Aslan welcomes the children and their friends into his country ('And as He spoke, He no longer looked to them like a lion'), and this is from the reader's point of view 'the end of all the stories'. But for the children themselves it is the beginning: all they have experienced is only 'the cover and the title page', and now the real story begins 'which no one on earth has ever read: which goes on for ever: in which every chapter is better than the one before' (p. 767).

Demystifying death

This brings us to what must be one of the most difficult subjects in the whole sequence of stories. Not many children's books end with the death of all the main characters (lovers of the film *The Muppet Treasure Island* will recall the reaction to the death of Captain Billy Bones: 'He died? I thought this was supposed to be a kids' movie'). As *Last Battle* unfolds, it becomes clear that the three Pevensie children, along with Polly, Digory, Eustace and Jill, have been

> Not many children's books end with the death of all the main characters

involved in a fatal train crash, which we are to understand has also killed the Pevensie parents. '"There was a real railway accident," said Aslan softly. "Your father and mother and all of you are – as you used to call it in the Shadowlands – dead"' (p. 767).

Once again, this has aroused indignation among some critical readers. Doesn't it indicate that, ultimately, Lewis is a 'world-denying' writer, who rather than allow his characters ordinary adult lives kills them off and dispatches them to a land of fantasy? Put in those terms, the charge is nonsense, for all the reasons we have already spelled out. But there is undoubtedly a challenge in a narrative climax involving a small holocaust of major characters.[5] This ending, however, is entirely of a piece with some of Lewis's most familiar themes throughout, which can be summarized as an attempt to *demystify* death. As already noted in Chapter 1, there is a fair amount of violent death around in the books, of the sort you regularly meet in folk- and fairy-tales and in old-fashioned adventure stories. Battles and single combat may entail death, and it is taken for granted that Narnia is a world in which there is such a thing as honourable (if not exactly virtuous) killing as well as honourable risking of death. The ethics of this world are the ethics of 'traditional' societies, including the mediaeval Christendom in which Lewis generally felt so much at home. Difficult as this may be, it does not – as again we noted earlier – necessarily involve a glorification or sentimentalizing of violent death or violence in general.

If we start thinking of what the transition between the world of a twentieth-century child and that of a pre-modern militarized aristocracy (which is what Narnian society rests upon) might mean, there are moral problems galore; and we may well feel that Lewis is pretty cavalier in the relative ease with which he allows his children to acclimatize to Arthurian bloodshed. But there is no point in being too fastidious about what is after all the common coin of so many adventure narratives. Focusing on these reservations will blind us to what Lewis is most concerned with, time and again, in the stories, which is to remind us that death is not the worst thing that can happen. As Lewis's diabolical commentator Screwtape writes,[6] human beings 'of course, tend to regard death as the prime evil and survival

> *Death is not the worst thing that can happen*

as the greatest good'. And – to come at it from another direction much signposted in the stories – it is the passion to avoid death at all costs that is commonly the root of the worst evils. Jadis desires immortality and achieves it, or something very like it; and it turns out to be hell. The other side of the coin to the apparently blithe acceptance of violent death is a taking for granted that there are worse things than death – a point you can, after all, find in the Gospels (Matthew 10.28: 'Do not be afraid of those who kill the body but cannot kill the soul'). And among those worse things is the breaking of faith: hence the difficult episode in *Magician's Nephew* that we discussed earlier, where Digory is sent by Aslan to fetch the apple from the paradisal garden at the far end of the world. Digory's miserable and stubborn obedience to Aslan carries in it the implicit recognition that his first task is to be true to what he has promised, even if it means risking not his life but his mother's. As Aslan explains to him, the breaking of his promise would make any other outcome an empty and destructive affair.

I suspect, incidentally, that this echoes very particularly an episode in Malory's *Morte d'Arthur*, where, in the context of the quest for the Holy Grail, one of the knights on the quest is tested in a similar way, by being faced with an apparent choice between betraying his marriage vows and letting someone die. Like Digory, he acts on the assumption that a broken vow would infect any possible result. It is a perspective that will be deeply uncomfortable to practically all contemporary readers (it is what makes Shakespeare's *Measure for Measure* so problematic for us).[7] But there is no point in softening it. The merits of the specific cases used by Lewis or Malory or even Shakespeare to put the point may not be universally agreed; but the underlying challenge is profoundly serious. There is a basic issue about the inseparability of means and ends; if we cannot recognize why this is serious, our ethical thinking is in a mess.

Death is part of a moral landscape. It is seen from a perspective that takes for granted a conviction of human dignity that death cannot erase. His colleague Nevill Coghill quotes Lewis's response to a question about the hydrogen bomb, Lewis pointing out the obvious fact that a substantial portion of the human race had spent centuries living in the expectation of the imminent and painful end of the world, and adding that 'when the bomb falls there will always be just that split second in which one can say, "Pooh! You're only a bomb. I'm an immortal soul."'[8] This is not airy dismissal of a real threat (as we have seen, Lewis was quite capable of analysing the moral nonsense of the arms race), but evidence of a firm sense of proportion. The threat is terrible but not unique;

and no level of threat should make you question your – and your neighbour's – value in the sight of your Maker.

Our habitual embarrassment about death is nicely caught in the exchange – towards the end of *Silver Chair* (Ch. 16, pp. 661–2) – between Aslan, Eustace and Caspian. Caspian is restored to life (and youth) by the blood shed from Aslan's paw as Eustace, at Aslan's command, drives a thorn into it. But Eustace cannot quite believe what has happened.

> 'But,' said Eustace, looking at Aslan. 'Hasn't he – er – died?'
>
> 'Yes,' said the Lion in a very quiet voice, almost (Jill thought) as if he were laughing. 'He has died. Most people have, you know. Even I have.'

Almost laughing; because what is in focus here is the human unwillingness to face both the fact of death and the fact of resurrection (resurrection, we should notice, at the cost of Aslan's suffering). But elsewhere there is a slightly different emotional colouring. When in *Magician's Nephew* (Ch. 12) Digory pleads with Aslan to help his dying mother, he is surprised to see tears in Aslan's eyes,

> such big, bright tears compared with Digory's own that for a moment he felt as if the Lion must really be sorrier about his Mother than he was himself.
>
> 'My son, my son,' said Aslan. 'I know. Grief is great. Only you and I in this land know that yet. Let us be good to one another.' (p. 83)

Human loss is not trivial, death is not nothing; and it is a powerful stroke of imagination to put divinity and humanity together for this brief moment at the dawn of Narnia as the only kinds of life that know about pain. Indeed, the moral issue over whether there are things worse than death would not be as acute as it is if loss and mortality and the sheer terror of suffering were not as they are. It is always worth recalling that Lewis fought in the trenches; he was not prone to minimizing these things.

The end of all endings

Death is profoundly serious, yet less than final. 'The view that death is a hideous enemy is not unscriptural, you know,' Lewis wrote to a priest in the USA in 1961, 'much less so than all the blab about there "being no death" or "death not matter-ing".'[9] And it is, of course, the gateway to an intensification of what has been life-giving here. In comparison with what lies ahead, the most vivid experiences of this world will seem dreamlike. We have seen already the way in which life beyond death is pictured as an endlessly unfolding story; we could say that, for Lewis, the salient point about death was that it put an end

Life beyond death is pictured as an endlessly unfolding story

to 'endings' and opened up this perspective of growth without a final horizon. In the final chapter of *Dawn Treader* – a poignantly dreamlike sequence of images – we travel with Caspian and the children to the very end of the world,

> and when the third day dawned . . . they saw a wonder ahead. It was as if a wall stood up between them and the sky, a greenish-grey, shimmering, trembling wall . . . a long tall wave – a wave endlessly fixed in one place as you may often see at the edge of a waterfall.   (p. 539)

This wave, translucent to the sun behind it and to a mountain landscape 'beyond the sun', is the veil that represents the frontier between Narnia and 'Aslan's country'; and it is a potent image of something like endlessly suspended desire; as if that suspension of fulfilment is precisely where we sense the border between this world and God's. 'A smell and a sound, a musical sound' reach them. 'Edmund and Eustace would never talk about it afterwards. Lucy could only say, "It would break your heart." "Why?" said I, "Was it so sad?" "Sad!! No," said Lucy.'

Reepicheep the mouse presses on up towards the crest of the wave and disappears. The others wade along the edge of the wave until they reach a level plain of grass where the sun seems to meet the sky; and there is a lamb, inviting them to have breakfast: 'there was a fire lit on the grass and fish roasting on it' (p. 540). This is another of Lewis's infrequent direct allusions to the text of the Bible, to the last chapter of John's Gospel where the risen Jesus meets the disciples at the lakeside and prepares a breakfast of fish roasted on a fire. The children are about to be sent back to their own world and are told that it is there that they will have to find the gateway to Aslan's country: it is as though the imagery of this episode is deliberately designed to prepare us for the story we shall indeed encounter in our own world, the story of the Resurrection of the slaughtered Lamb. In our world, says Aslan, 'I have another name. You must learn to know me by that name' (p. 541). We are being alerted to the identity of the Lion and the Lamb in the imagery of Christian Scripture, and to the fact that the Resurrection of the Lamb is in our world the gateway to Aslan's world. When, in *Last Battle*, Lucy reminds the others that a stable in their world once contained something greater than that entire world, we can conclude that Lucy at least has learned to know Aslan by another name.[10] And her reply to the narrator's question – 'Sad!! No' – is as eloquent a witness as any there could be to what we can expect in the light of the Resurrection; a breaking of the heart that brings unbearable delight.

> *The Resurrection of the Lamb is in our world the gateway to Aslan's world*

The familiar world has to be broken open by the life it contains in order for joy to be full. Death is the climax of that breaking open, just as every particular meeting with Aslan face to face is part of it. The price of moving into this interior world that is greater than the exterior is high – but not too high for what it promises. In a famous and vivid passage in *The Screwtape Letters*,[11] the devilish author explodes in disgust at the enemy's obsession with joy:

> He's a hedonist at heart. All those fasts and vigils and stakes and crosses are only a facade . . . Out at sea, out in His sea, there is pleasure, and more pleasure . . . He has a bourgeois mind. He has filled His world full of pleasures. There are things for humans to do all day long without His minding in the least.

Part of Lewis's success in the Narnia books is to evoke both the cost and the pleasure.

There is one final point worth making about the imagery of the immeasurable 'inside' breaking the 'outside' mould. Lewis does not labour this point, but Lucy's allusion to the stable of Bethlehem in *Last Battle* should remind us of just how pervasive in Christian language such a picture is. The Incarnation is often spoken of, not least in Christian poetry, as the containing of the uncontainable: 'In this rose contained was Heaven and earth in little space', in the words of the mediaeval carol; or John Donne's 'Eternity cloister'd in thy dear womb.' The bread and wine of the Eucharist are likewise seen as embodying and carrying the infinitely greater reality of the act and presence of Christ in his full humanity and divinity. There is a tradition (not least in the Eastern Christian world once again) that prefers to speak of the body as 'within' the soul rather than the other way round. And there is a lot to be said for understanding the Church itself as bigger on the inside than the outside, with all that might mean for the priorities of Christian life: what matters most is not necessarily the figure that the Church cuts in the world but what is transformingly going on in the shared life of its members – which won't lend itself much to sound bites or dramatic images a lot of the time.

In all these instances, it is essential to remember that the 'container' never becomes insignificant, and is never simply denied. It has a *share* in what it contains, it is not just a veil thrown over to hide the reality. The humanity of Christ is not abolished by its glorification in the Ascension; the body shares in the 'overflow' of glory from the soul (the language is that of St Thomas Aquinas); the material form of the sacrament is (for most Christians) to be appropriately

> *The humanity of Christ is not abolished by its glorification in the Ascension*

venerated, though there may be disagreement about what 'appropriate' means; the Church needs to be loved and served in its actual and tangible form, not just in some 'invisible' perfection. Lewis's world view is emphatically that of a wide swathe of Christian tradition, East and West, in denying that the vehicles of God's revelation are unimportant and detached from the reality they convey. Against a theology that assumes an unbridgeable divide between grace and nature, let alone matter and spirit, Lewis defends the belief that what is created can be infused by the uncreated act of God and so given depth and dignity. Ultimately, the imagery of the wardrobe and the stable, standing at the beginning and the conclusion of the Narnia stories like bookends, is there to say something substantial about the whole relation of God to the world, the human Jesus to the divine Word, the body to the soul, the inexhaustible character of human identity itself.

Conclusion

Narnia brings into clear focus a wide variety of central Christian themes; but out of this variety there are at least three that seem to emerge particularly strongly from the discussion in these pages. If, as I suggested at the beginning, Lewis's aim is to help us sense what the experience of God is 'like', as if we had never before really thought about it, one of the main things he achieves is a sort of redefinition of 'transcendence'. The word as normally used brings to mind pictures of distance: the transcendent is what is unattainably far off, outside our range of understanding. But Lewis, like the best of Christian theologians throughout the centuries, helps us see that what matters is not distance but difference; not an incalculable separation but an inexhaustible strangeness, a refusal to be captured. And in Lewis's narrative, this is expressed in terms of rebellion, the joyful overturning of a self-contained order in the name of an uncontainable *Transcendence is the wildness of joy* truth. Transcendence is the wildness of joy; and the truth of God becomes a revolution against what we have made of ourselves. Like Chesterton's characters, we are all given the opportunity of the romance of being rebels. Evil is cast as the ultimate force of reaction; we are invited to see ourselves as living 'under occupation' and summoned to join a resistance movement. The recognition of transcendence becomes the knowledge that there is life beyond the drab 'Soviet' world of limited possibilities and carefully prescribed duties.

So far, so good; it is exhilarating to think of ourselves not just as victims of oppression but as active rebels against it. The catch comes with the second major insight that Narnia offers. *We* are the occupying forces. We have enslaved ourselves. So before we congratulate ourselves on joining the rebel troops, we need to confront the fact that what we are rebelling against is what we have voted for – and are still voting for. We are being invited to a revolution against what

> *What we are rebelling against is what we have voted for*

we have fairly consistently thought we wanted and who we fairly consistently thought we were. We shall be able to sustain our rebellion only if we have a robust new sense of who we just might be. And this can only be provided from beyond our own imagination and self-examination. It is good and necessary to question ourselves, of course; but it only opens new doors if we know what it is that could be different. To learn this, we must be engaged in conversation with a highly dangerous stranger; how we come to trust him, in spite of everything, is a long story, and one whose details will vary greatly from person to person. But it will have something to do with the conviction that we can 'safely' (not quite the right word) confront our own untruthfulness in the stranger's presence because this stranger will not simply condemn or walk away. To know this is to feel the first beginnings of what release from our 'occupied' condition might mean and feel like.

Hence to the third moment. When we are finally liberated from the occupation, what lies before us is an unending journey into light and joy: we are at last radically opened up to the largely lost possibility of really self-forgetting enjoyment, so vivid and solid is what we are able to experience. The vision of a new world is one in which both I and my environment acquire a *depth* hitherto unimaginable. Both persons and the world in which they live become manifestly worth taking unlimited time over; and that unlimited time is guaranteed. What we are now encountering is the connectedness of all that is around us to its inexhaustible root or ground in the divine – the connectedness of the various mountain spurs to the central

> *We are at last radically opened up to the largely lost possibility of really self-forgetting enjoyment*

massif of Aslan's country. The encounter with unqualified truth and love that is involved in meeting Aslan has the effect of making everything 'more like the real thing', more compelling of our love and delight. Conversely – and soberingly – walking away from this encounter because we are afraid of its cost will take us inexorably back towards the boredom and imprisonment of ourselves – back to the occupied territory of a self too concerned to defend its boundaries to be able to contemplate joy.

In a word, what Lewis portrays with such power and fresh-ness in Narnia is simply *grace*: the unplanned and uncon-trolled incursion into our self-preoccupied lives of God's joy in himself. *Surprised by Joy* is more than the title of an autobiography. It is a summary of what Lewis most wanted to convey, recognizing as he did that once you had begun to understand this, all sorts of *details* of Christian doctrine would fall into place – the nature of repentance as both gift and demand, the possibility of a transfiguring of the mater-ial order, the unchangeable character of God as something that necessarily goes with his freedom to be involved in the totally different life of created beings, the inseparability of knowledge and love in God, and so on. All these ideas and

> In a word, what Lewis portrays with such power and freshness in Narnia is simply **grace**

many more could be worked out from a close reading of the Narnia stories. But it is not much use trying to arrive at what might be called the Narnian experience if you begin from these principles. It can't be said too often that the abstractions of theology and the conceptual tangles and apparent contradictions that arise so frequently are the result of searching for language that will do justice to a new sense of what is possible. The more we are preoccupied with the tangles, the more we are likely to have lost sight of that sense of the possible. We can't renew it just by trying hard. We can at least put ourselves in the way of rediscovering it by letting down the guard of our imagination from time to time.

When the children are sent back to their own world at the very end of *Dawn Treader* (an end that, as we have seen, is exceptionally charged and poignant: 'Sad!! No'), Lucy protests:

> 'It isn't Narnia, you know,' sobbed Lucy. 'It's you. We shan't meet you there. And how can we live, never meeting you?'
>
> 'But you shall meet me, dear one,' said Aslan.
>
> 'Are – are you there too, Sir?' said Edmund.
>
> 'I am,' said Aslan. 'But there I have another name. You must learn to know me by that name. This was the very reason why you were brought to Narnia, that by knowing me here for a little, you may know me better there.'   (p. 541)

The reader is brought to Narnia for a little in order to know Aslan better in this world. All that we have been trying to do in these pages is to make sure that the doors between the worlds are in reasonably good order, so that we may share that slowly flowering awareness of something constantly discovered and rediscovered and always new. Stella Gibbons, in an essay I have quoted several times, speaks of the shock of finding on the last page of *Last Battle* 'the great lion . . . given a capital H – "and as He spoke to them, He no longer looked like a lion"': 'pure shock, as if cold water had spouted up from the page.'[1] Lewis could have asked no better reaction than such a shock, the shock of unexpected homecoming as the Lion's world is revealed once and for all as our own.

Notes

CL I, II and III refer to Lewis's *Collected Letters*, volumes I (1905–31), II (1931–49) and III (1950–63), edited by Walter Hooper, London, HarperCollins, 2000, 2004 and 2006.

Preface

1 For a moving evocation of the intense – embarrassingly and confusingly intense – effect of the Narnia stories, see Francis Spufford, *The Child that Books Built: A memoir of childhood and reading*, London, Faber and Faber, 2002, pp. 87–107; possibly the best account of this to have been written, all the stronger for being open-eyed about Lewis's prejudices and limitations.

2 *The Cambridge Companion to C. S. Lewis*, edited by Robert MacSwain and Michael Ward, Cambridge, Cambridge University Press, 2010, including pieces by luminaries like Alan Jacobs, Kevin Vanhoozer and Stanley Hauerwas.

3 For references to Merton, see CL III, p. 380 (apparently defending Merton's defence of the contemplative life against a critic who was accusing Merton of rejecting the world), pp. 1304–5 (describing Merton's *No Man is an Island* as 'the best new spiritual reading I've met for a long time') and p. 1307.

4 A. N. Wilson's *C. S. Lewis: A biography*, London, Collins, 1990, offended many devotees, but it is a major contribution to such a three-dimensional picture. Many of the judgements here are certainly open to debate, but I don't think that Lewis emerges in any way *diminished* by the portrait.

Introduction

1 William Griffin, *C. S. Lewis: The authentic voice*, Tring, Lion, 2005, p. 329.

2 Michael Ward, *Planet Narnia: The seven heavens in the imagination of C. S. Lewis*, New York and Oxford, Oxford University Press, 2008.

3 CL III, pp. 847–8.

4 CL III, p. 1113.

5 CL III, p. 1113; cf. the letters to Patricia Mackey (pp. 1157–8) and Anne Jenkins (pp. 1244–5).

1 The point of Narnia

1 Pullman's most uncompromising declaration of war can be found in his article 'The Dark Side of Narnia' in the London *Guardian* for 1 October 1998, <http://reports.guardian.co.uk/articles/1998/10/1/p-24747.html. For a full bibliography, see Steven Barfield and Katherine Cox, eds, *Critical Perspectives on Philip Pullman's* His Dark Materials: *Essays on the novels, the film and the stage productions*, Jefferson, NC, and London, McFarland, 2011.

2 John Goldthwaite, *The Natural History of Make-Believe: A guide to the principal works of Britain, Europe and America*, New York and Oxford, Oxford University Press, 1996, pp. 232–3. The unexpectedly personal intensity of Goldthwaite's assault on Lewis has been noted by a good many readers, and there is an insightful discussion of his treatment in 'Constructions of the Child, Authority and Authorship' by Elisabeth Eldridge, pp. 40–56 in Barfield and Cox, *Critical Perspectives*. A. N. Wilson, *C. S. Lewis: A biography*, London, Collins, 1990, p. 226, likewise presents Puddleglum's argument with the Witch in *Silver Chair* as 'a nursery nightmare version of Lewis's debate with Miss Anscombe'.

3 See, for example, Alan Jacobs, 'The Chronicles of Narnia', pp. 265–80 in *The Cambridge Companion to C. S. Lewis*, edited by Robert MacSwain and Michael Ward, Cambridge, Cambridge University Press, 2010, pp. 265–6.

4 The traumatic impact of the Anscombe debate may have been overstated (not to say preposterously exaggerated, as in Goldthwaite's *Natural History*). Lewis subsequently revised the text of his book on miracles to take account

of Anscombe's critique, and there is no evidence that he bore any personal animosity towards Anscombe. For some sensible remarks, see Alan Jacobs, 'The Chronicles of Narnia', pp. 266–7; and n.b. Francis Spufford, *The Child that Books Built: A memoir of childhood and reading*, London, Faber and Faber, 2002, p. 98, who notes that Anscombe herself did not think Lewis particularly upset by the debate.

5 CL III, p. 93.

6 On the genesis of ideas for Narnia, see Jacobs, 'The Chronicles of Narnia', p. 267, referring to Lewis's 1960 *Radio Times* article, 'It All Began with a Picture'.

7 CL II, p. 683.

8 See the comments in *Surprised by Joy*, London, Geoffrey Bles, 1955 and Collins (Fontana Books) 1959, p. 154; cf. pp. 180–1.

9 See *The Letters of Dorothy L. Sayers, vol. II, 1937–1943: From novelist to playwright*, edited by Barbara Reynolds, London, The Dorothy L. Sayers Society, 1997, for the bulk of her correspondence on this question.

10 Michael Ward, *Planet Narnia: The seven heavens in the imagination of C. S. Lewis*, New York and Oxford, Oxford University Press, 2008; and below, Chapter 3, n. 4, on Goldthwaite's objections.

11 CL III, p. 1265, for the phrase; and cf. Wilson, *C. S. Lewis*, p. 233, 'a sort of sluicing of the system'.

2 Narnia and its critics

1 Above, Chapter 1, n. 1, and see the various discussions in Steven Barfield and Katherine Cox, eds, *Critical Perspectives on Philip Pullman's His Dark Materials: Essays on the novels, the film and the stage productions*, Jefferson, NC, and London, McFarland, 2011, Section 1, 'Adversaries and Influences'.

2 John Goldthwaite, *The Natural History of Make-Believe: A guide to the principal works of Britain, Europe and America*, New York and Oxford, Oxford University Press, 1996, pp. 220–44; a sustained and quite convoluted theological as well as moral critique, coming to the bizarre conclusion

that Lewis, along with Tolkien, is (or is colluding with those who are) both fundamentalist and Gnostic in expressing 'a discontent with God for the state of His world' (p. 243), and 'an itch for power and a mistrust of God' (p. 244).

3 CL II, pp. 70–1; *Surprised by Joy*, London, Geoffrey Bles, 1955 and Collins (Fontana Books) 1959, p. 188. On literary 'orientalism' in Narnia, see Judith Wolfe, 'On Power', pp. 174–88 in *The Cambridge Companion to C. S. Lewis*, edited by Robert MacSwain and Michael Ward, Cambridge, Cambridge University Press, 2010, p. 179 – with the qualifications on p. 184, so that Lewis is not unconditionally absolved of 'prejudice and insensitivity' in this area.

4 CL III, pp. 408, 703–4. The latter intriguingly echoes the kind of imagery found at the end of *Last Battle*.

> Further knowledge would leave our map of, say, the Atlantic quite *correct*, but if it turned out to be the estuary of a great river – and the continent thro' wh. that river flowed turned out to be itself an island – off the shores of a still greater continent – and so on! You see what I mean? Not one jot of Revelation will be proved false: but so many new truths might be added.

5 In Jocelyn Gibb, ed. *Light on C. S. Lewis*, London, Geoffrey Bles, 1965, p. 93.

6 CL III, pp. 1135–6.

7 Stella Gibbons in Gibb, ed. *Light on C. S. Lewis*, p. 93.

8 Goldthwaite, *Natural History*, p. 241.

9 'On violence', *Cambridge Companion*, pp. 189–202.

3 Not a tame lion

1 *Surprised by Joy*, London, Geoffrey Bles, 1955 and Collins (Fontana Books) 1959, pp. 94–5; this is echoed in some of the poems in Lewis's pre-conversion collection of poems, *Spirits in Bondage*, London, Harcourt, Brace and Javanovich, 1919.

2 CL II, p. 501.

3 *That Hideous Strength: A modern fairy-tale for grown-ups*, London, Bodley Head, 1945 and HarperCollins, 2005, pp. 467–8.

4 John Goldthwaite, *The Natural History of Make-Believe: A guide to the principal works of Britain, Europe and America*, New York and Oxford, Oxford University Press, 1996, castigates Lewis for his selectivity both in welcoming some but not all the personages of Greek mythology and in apparently approving aspects of Greek paganism while rejecting contemporary non-Christian faiths.

5 *That Hideous Strength*, pp. 421–2, 435–6.

6 *A Grief Observed*, London, Faber and Faber, 1961, p. 10.

7 See Joseph Frank, *Dostoevsky: The mantle of the prophet, 1871–1881*, Princeton, Princeton University Press, 2002, pp. 712–13; and cf. Rowan Williams, *Dostoevsky: Language, faith and fiction*, Waco, TX, Baylor University Press and London, Continuum, 2008, pp. 44–5.

8 *A Grief Observed*, pp. 26–7.

9 Joseph Frank, *Dostoevsky*, p. 712; Williams, *Dostoevsky*, p. 15 and Ch. 1 passim.

10 Pullman and others have argued that this incident does imply a sort of threat, making it a sadistically manipulative tactic on Aslan's part.

4 No story but your own

1 In Jocelyn Gibb, ed. *Light on C. S. Lewis*, London, Geoffrey Bles, 1965, p. xvi.

2 *Surprised by Joy*, London, Geoffrey Bles, 1955 and Collins (Fontana Books) 1959, p. 186.

3 Gibb, ed. *Light on C. S. Lewis*, p. xi.

4 CL I, p. 819–21 (W. H. Lewis, *Letters of C. S. Lewis*, London, Geoffrey Bles, 1966, pp. 136–8).

5 Cf. William Griffin, *C. S. Lewis: The authentic voice*, Tring, Lion, 2005, p. 329. A. N. Wilson, *C. S. Lewis: A biography*, London, Collins, 1990, p. 225, underlines the 'signs of extraordinary haste' in the composition of the books, including inconsistencies and (untypical) slackness in writing.

6 See particularly *The Great Divorce*, London, Geoffrey Bles, 1946 and Collins (Fontana Books), 1972, pp. 99–205. It is worth noting how Francis Spufford remembers his reaction as a child to Eustace's experience:

> The books pressed a question, insistently: are you willing to be transformed? . . . I'm sure reading the books now (and I was sure then, though I wouldn't have put the thought into words) that there was nothing manipulative or Machiavellian about Lewis's belief in Aslan's claws. He didn't urge anything on you that he didn't think he needed himself.
>
> (Francis Spufford, *The Child that Books Built: A memoir of childhood and reading*, London, Faber and Faber, 2002, pp. 104–5)

7 CL III, p. 429.

8 *That Hideous Strength: A modern fairy-tale for grown-ups*, London, Bodley Head, 1945 and HarperCollins 2005, pp. 236–7.

5 The silent gaze of truth

1 See, e.g. *The Great Divorce*, London, Geoffrey Bles, 1946 and Collins (Fontana Books), 1972, pp. 103–9, for a struggle over what is left of a chronically self-dramatizing and self-pitying soul:

> One could see an unheard-of idea trying to enter his little mind: one could even see that there was for him some sweetness in it. For a second he almost let the chain go . . . I do not know that I ever saw anything more terrible than the struggle of that Dwarf Ghost against joy . . . But the light that reached him, reached him against his will. This was not the meeting he had pictured; he would not accept it. (pp. 103, 106)

2 *That Hideous Strength: A modern fairy-tale for grown-ups*, London, Bodley Head, 1945 and HarperCollins, 2005, p. 499.

3 Stanley Cavell, *Disowning Knowledge in Seven Plays of Shakespeare*, Cambridge, Cambridge University Press, 2003 (updated edition), Ch. 3, 'Othello and the Stake of the Other'.

4 CL III, p. 429.

6 Bigger inside than outside

1 For a lucid introduction to Maximus' work, see Lars Thunberg, *Man and the Cosmos: The vision of St Maximus the Confessor*, Crestwood, NY, St Vladimir's Seminary Press, 1985, especially Ch. 7, pp. 132–7.

2 The literature on the relations between Lewis and Williams is vast. For a good brief introduction to Williams' thought, see Charles Hefling, 'Charles Williams: Words, images and (the) Incarnation' in David Hein and Edward Henderson, eds, *C. S. Lewis and Friends*, London, SPCK, 2011, pp. 73–90. Williams' essay on 'The Way of Affirmation' can be found in the posthumous collection of his work, *The Image of the City, and Other Essays*, ed. Anne Ridler, London, Oxford University Press, 1958.

3 *The Great Divorce*, London, Geoffrey Bles, 1946 and Collins (Fontana Books), 1972, pp. 27, 117–18.

4 *That Hideous Strength: A modern fairy-tale for grown-ups*, London, Bodley Head, 1945 and HarperCollins, 2005, p. 517.

5 Pullman, in his *Guardian* article, 1 October 1998, <http://reports.guardian.co.uk/articles/1998/10/1/p-24747.html>, points to this as evidence of a 'life-hating ideology'. A more complex reaction can be found in a story by a contemporary writer of fantasy who builds his narrative around the trauma for Susan of losing her entire family in a single catastrophe: see Neil Gaiman, 'The Problem of Susan', in *Flights: Extreme visions of fantasy* vol. II, ed. Al Sarrantonio, New York, New American Library, 2004.

6 *The Screwtape Letters: Letters from a senior to a junior devil*, London, Geoffrey Bles, 1942 and Collins (Fontana Books), 1955, no. xxviii, p. 142.

7 Lewis would not necessarily have sympathized with such difficulties. In 1940, he writes approvingly to Bede Griffiths about R. W. Chambers' essay on *Measure for Measure* as 'an ordinary Christian story' (CL II, pp. 326–7).

8 In Jocelyn Gibb, ed. *Light on C. S. Lewis*, London, Geoffrey Bles, 1965, pp. 64–5.

9 CL III, pp. 1245–6.

10 CL III, p. 744 ('As to whether they knew their Creed, I suppose Professor Kirke and the Lady Polly and the Pevensies did, but probably Eustace and Pole, who had been brought up at that rotten school, did *not*').

11 *The Screwtape Letters: Letters from a senior to a junior devil*, London, Geoffrey Bles, 1942 and Collins (Fontana Books), 1955, no. xxii, p. 112; and cf. Francis Spufford, *The Child that Books Built: A memoir of childhood and reading*, London, Faber and Faber, 2002, pp. 95–6, for a dazzling elaboration of the metaphor.

Conclusion

1 In Jocelyn Gibb, ed. *Light on C. S. Lewis*, London, Geoffrey Bles, 1965, p. 100.